Typing
for everyone

By NATHAN LEVINE

B. S. in Ed.

Former teacher of Gregg Shorthand and Typing
New York City Public Day and Evening High Schools

ARCO PUBLISHING, INC.
219 Park Avenue South, New York, N.Y. 10003

4-MINUTE SCORE SHEET

Best Speed within 4 errors:		LESSONS				
		26	27	28	29	30
Goal:	22					
	21					
	20					
	19					
	18					
	17					
	16					
	15					
	14					
	13					
	12					
	11					
	10					

5-MINUTE SCORE SHEET

Best Speed within 5 errors:		LESSONS				
		31	32	33	34	35
Goal:	25					
	24					
	23					
	22					
	21					
	20					
	19					
	18					
	17					
	16					
	15					
	14					
	13					
	12					
	11					
	10					

CONTENTS

1. ALPHABET, SHIFT KEYS, SHIFT LOCK *Page*

A S D F J K L 10
E U 14
R I 16
G O 18
Shift Keys 20
T H 22
W Y 24
Q P 26
C V 31
B M X 33
Z N 35
Shift Lock 37

2. PUNCTUATION MARKS

.   (Period) 20
,   (Comma) 24
;   (Semicolon) 10
:   (Colon) 26
?   (Question Mark) 35
-   (Hyphen) 37
-- (Dash) 38
'   (Apostrophe) 58
!   (Exclamation Mark) 58

3. FIGURES and FRACTIONS

1   3   7 41
2   6 43
5   9 45
4   8   0 47
½ 56
¼ 66

4. SYMBOLS

/   (Slant) 31
¢   (Cents) 56
$ (Dollars) 58
&   (Ampersand) 60
%   (Per Cent) 62
_   (Underscore) 64
(Number or Pounds) 60
( ) (Parentheses) 62
"   (Quotation Mark) 64
@   (At or Per) 66
*   (Asterisk) 66

5. SKILL BUILDERS

A. Accuracy: Paragraph Practice .... Lessons 9-26
B. Speed: 1-Minute Timings .... Lessons 6-14
             2-Minute Timings .... Lessons 15-20
             3-Minute Timings .... Lessons 21-25
             4-Minute Timings .... Lessons 26-30
             5-Minute Timings .... Lessons 31-35

6. CENTERING *Page*

Horizontal 49
Vertical 52

7. LETTERS

Personal 69
Personal Business 73
Business 77

8. LISTINGS 89

9. TABULATIONS 93

10. TYPING AIDS

Keyboard Mastery Drills 108
Alphabetic Sentences 110
Speed Boosters 111
5-Minute Timed Tests 112
Common Errors in Machine Operation 118

Special Symbols 119
Typing on Lines 121
Aligning 122
Erasing 123
Crowding 124

Spreading 125
Pivoting 125
Carbon Copies 126
Manuscript Typing 127
Typing a Stencil 129

Rules for Word Division 130
Rules for Punctuation 131
Rules for Capitalization 138
Rules for Punctuation Spacing 141
Rules for Typing Numbers 142

General Spelling Rules 144

Addressing Envelopes and Postal Cards 148
New State Abbreviations 149
Addressing Very Large Envelopes 149
"Chainfeeding" Envelopes 150
Typing Postal Cards 150

Folding and Inserting a Letter 151
Special Forms of Address, Salutation, and
Complimentary Close 153
Proofreading Marks 156
Roman Numerals 158
Timed Typing Score Sheets 159-160

1-MINUTE SCORE SHEET

Best Speed within 3 errors:

LESSONS

		6	7	8	9	10	11	12	13	14
Goal:	15									
	14									
	13									
	12									
	11									
	10									
	9									
	8									
	7									
	6									

2-MINUTE SCORE SHEET

Best Speed within 4 errors:

LESSONS

		15	16	17	18	19	20
Goal:	18						
	17						
	16						
	15						
	14						
	13						
	12						
	11						
	10						

3-MINUTE SCORE SHEET

Best Speed within 4 errors:

LESSONS

		21	22	23	24	25
Goal:	20					
	19					
	18					
	17					
	16					
	15					
	14					
	13					
	12					
	11					
	10					

Here is a sample score sheet that shows you how to keep a record of all your timings.

Copy the form on graph paper and record your best speed in lesson 6 within 3 errors.

With lesson 7, you can start joining the scores and see your skill grow.

NOTE: If this is your own book, you may use the forms for the 2-3-4-5-minute timings on pages 159 and 160.

If this is a school or library book, do not write on these forms. Copy them on graph paper.

Score Sheet

Manual Typewriter

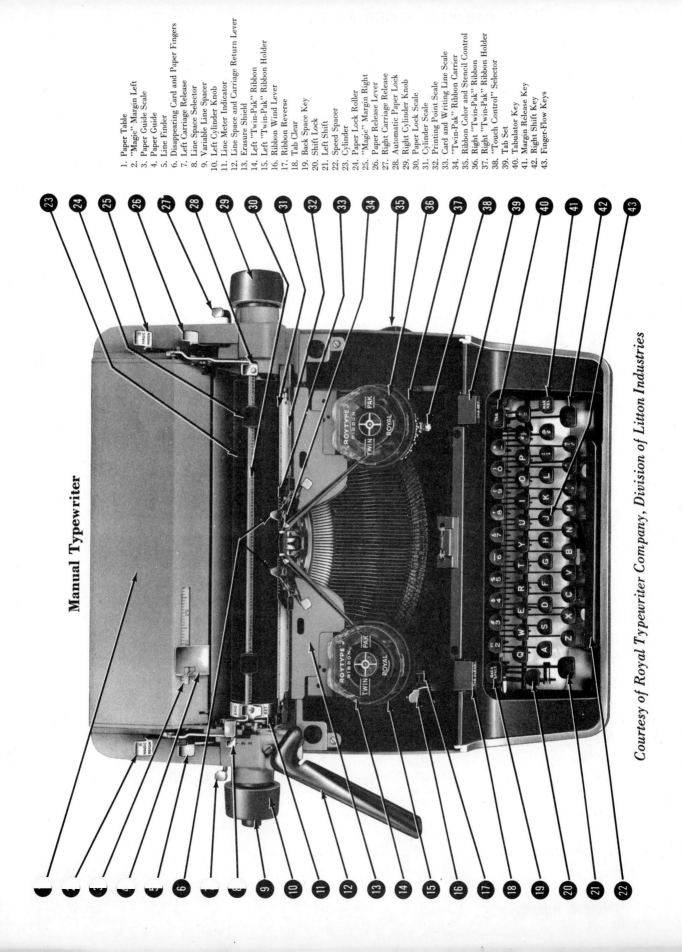

1. Paper Table
2. "Magic" Margin Left
3. Paper Guide Scale
4. Paper Guide
5. Line Finder
6. Disappearing Card and Paper Fingers
7. Left Carriage Release
8. Line Space Selector
9. Variable Line Spacer
10. Left Cylinder Knob
11. Line Meter Indicator
12. Line Space and Carriage Return Lever
13. Erasure Shield
14. Left "Twin-Pak" Ribbon
15. Left "Twin-Pak" Ribbon Holder
16. Ribbon Wind Lever
17. Ribbon Reverse
18. Tab Clear
19. Back Space Key
20. Shift Lock
21. Left Shift
22. Speed Spacer
23. Cylinder
24. Paper Lock Roller
25. "Magic" Margin Right
26. Paper Release Lever
27. Right Carriage Release
28. Automatic Paper Lock
29. Right Cylinder Knob
30. Paper Lock Scale
31. Cylinder Scale
32. Printing Point Scale
33. Card and Writing Line Scale
34. "Twin-Pak" Ribbon Carrier
35. Ribbon Color and Stencil Control
36. Right "Twin-Pak" Ribbon
37. Right "Twin-Pak" Ribbon Holder
38. "Touch Control" Selector
39. Tab Set
40. Tabulator Key
41. Margin Release Key
42. Right Shift Key
43. Finger-Flow Keys

Courtesy of Royal Typewriter Company, Division of Litton Industries

ROMAN NUMERALS

1	I	30	XXX
2	II	35	XXXV
3	III	40	XL
4	IV	50	L
5	V	60	LX
6	VI	70	LXX
7	VII	80	LXXX
8	VIII	90	XC
9	IX	100	C
10	X	200	CC
11	XI	300	CCC
12	XII	400	CD
13	XIII	500	D
14	XIV	600	DC
15	XV	700	DCC
16	XVI	800	DCCC
17	XVII	900	CM
18	XVIII	1000	M
19	XIX	1500	MD
20	XX	1800	MDCCC
21	XXI	1899	MDCCCXCIX
22	XXII	1920	MCMXX
23	XXIII	1950	MCML
24	XXIV	1959	MCMLIX
25	XXV	1978	MCMLXXVIII

READING GUIDES

1. A letter repeated repeats its value:

X	10
XX	20
XXX	30

2. One or more letters placed after a letter of greater value adds thereto:

VI	6
LX	60
MCC	1200

3. A letter placed before one of greater value subtracts therefrom:

IV	4
XC	90
CM	900

4. A line over one or more letters multiplies the value by 1,000.

$\overline{V}$	5,000
$\overline{X}$	10,000
$\overline{C}$	100,000
$\overline{M}$	1,000,000
$\overline{XV}$	15,000
$\overline{CLIX}$	159,000

Roman Numerals

Electric Typewriter

1. PAPER TABLE
2. PAPER GUIDE SCALE
3. PAPER GUIDE
4. PAPER LOCK ROLLERS
5. LEFT "MAGIC" MARGIN
6. LINE FINDER
7. LINE SPACE SELECTOR
8. LEFT CARRIAGE RELEASE
9. LEFT CYLINDER KNOB
10. VARIABLE LINE SPACER
11. LINE METER INDICATOR
12. LINE METER
13. CYLINDER SCALE
14. PRINTING POINT SCALE
15. TYPE BARS
16. RIBBON REVERSE
17. TAB CLEAR
18. ON-OFF POWER SWITCH
19. FINGER FLOW KEYS
20. TABULATOR
21. "TOUCH CONTROL"
22. SHIFT LOCK
23. LEFT SHIFT KEY
24. HALF SPACER

25. TRANSPARENT WRITING LINE SCALE
26. RULING GUIDE
4. PAPER LOCK ROLLERS
27. PAPER LOCK SCALE
28. RIGHT "MAGIC" MARGIN
29. PAPER RELEASE
30. CYLINDER
31. RIGHT CARRIAGE RELEASE
32. RIGHT CYLINDER KNOB
33. AUTOMATIC PAPER LOCK
34. MARGIN JUSTIFIER
35. "MAGIC MONITOR"
36. RIBBON CARRIER
37. "TWIN PAK" CARTRIDGE HOLDER
38. "TWIN PAK" RIBBON
39. RIBBON COLOR AND STENCIL CONTROL
40. MARGIN BYPASS
41. TAB SET
42. REPEAT UNDERSCORE AND HYPHEN KEY
43. BACK SPACER
44. IMPRESSION CONTROL
45. CARRIAGE RETURN, SINGLE AND REPEAT
46. RIGHT SHIFT KEY
47. SPACE BAR, SINGLE AND REPEAT

Courtesy of Royal Typewriter Company, Division of Litton Industries

After the corrections have been made, the copy on page 156 will read as follows:

If you are planning to go to work in an office after graduation from high school, take all the business subjects offered. Typing, shorthand, English, business arithmetic, and bookkeeping are essential for most office jobs. They help a _beginner_ get a good start in the business world. Try to EXCEL in them.

Test your aptitude for office work while you are in school. Take part in its administrative, clerical, and bookkeeping functions. Also, try to get an office job during vacations. Whatever business experience you can get will give you a good chance to find out first hand what office work is like.

So prepare now by taking advantage of your high school years to build a firm foundation for _success_.

TO THE BEGINNER

Typing for Everyone will teach you to type by touch—without looking at your fingers. These lessons "work." They were tested for ten years on 3,000 beginners, ages 14 to 70: students, clerks, cashiers, bookkeepers, sales people, nurses, technical assistants, workers in all sorts of jobs and occupations. All of them learned quickly and expertly how to type.

Type a lesson a day. Learn a few keys at a time; then as you practice words, sentences and paragraphs, your control of those keys becomes automatic. Before you know it, you are a touch typist.

Here are some of the special features you will like about this book:

1. **Entirely Self-Teaching:**
   Each lesson is short, simple, easy to master; it tells you plainly what to do and how to do it; it is your own private home tutor.

2. **Cumulative Review:**
   Beginning with Lesson 2, you review all the keys you have learned; you reinforce your control of those keys before you go on to the new ones. You can see your day-to-day progress toward your goal of typing mastery.

3. **Accuracy and Speed-Building in Same Lesson:**
   You get intensive accuracy and speed-building practice in the same lesson to develop your maximum typing skill. Interesting, flowing copy helps you reach specific goals.

4. **Word-Counted Material:**
   Sentences, paragraphs, 1 to 5-minute copy tests, tell you at a glance how many words you've typed in a given time.

5. **Timed-Typing Score Sheet:**
   A simple, easy-to-use score sheet for each group of 1, 2, 3, 4, 5-minute timed tests lets you see your day-to-day progress in speed-with-accuracy.

6. **Realistic Business Letter Placement:**
   No complicated scales to memorize. An all-purpose letter-placement formula tells you how to arrange quickly and attractively ALL styles of business letters.

7. **Simplified Tabulation:**
   No diagrams, no arithmetic. You learn the BACKSPACE way to type material in columns.

8. **Typing Aids:**
   Basic office "Know-Hows"—to help you become a proficient typist.

You may sometimes have to type a revised copy of typed or printed matter. Some notations indicating the corrections will be self-explanatory; others will consist of special symbols known as proofreading marks. These symbols are often used by writers, editors, and businessmen. Each correction is indicated in the copy and in the margin, left or right. Some of the more common symbols are illustrated below.

¶	Paragraph	#	Leave a space	⊙	Insert period
≡	Capital Letter	[	Move to Left	⌃	Insert comma
Caps	All capitals	]	Move to right	⌃	Insert semicolon
tr	Transpose	*lc*	Small letter	?	Insert question mark
ℐ	Take it out	⊔	Lower this letter	!	Insert exclamation mark
stet	Don't change	⊓	Raise this letter	*ital*	Set in italics
		◯	Close up		

Placing Proofreading Marks

¶ If you are planning to go ~~directly~~ to work in an office ℐ

after graduation from high school, ta~~ek~~ all the business *tr*

≡ subjects offered. ~~T~~yping, shorthand, English, ~~B~~usiness *l.c.*

⌃ arithmetic‚ and bookkeeping are essential for most office

underscore jobs. They help a beginner get a good start in the busi-

caps ness world. Try to ~~excel~~ in ~~these subjects~~. *them*

    Test your aptitude for office work while you are in

school. Take part in its ~~administrative~~, clerical, and *stet*

[[bookkeeping functions. Also, try to get an office job

]]during vacations. Whatever ~~b~~usiness experience you can get ⊔

◯ will give you a good ch‿ance to find out first hand ⊓hat ⊓
              w

⊙ office work is like⌃

So‿prepare now by taking advantage of your high

school years to build a firm foundation for success. *ital*

STEP 1: PREPARE YOUR TYPEWRITER

Before you begin a lesson, follow this routine:

1. **Set the Paper Guide at "0" on the Paper Guide Scale.**

   A. The paper guide is a blade at the left end of the carriage.

   B. Slide the blade left or right until its edge points to "0" on the paper-guide scale.

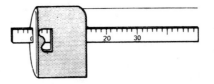

Fig. 1. Paper Guide at "0"

2. **Set the Line-Space Regulator at "1" for Single Spacing.**

   A. The line-space regulator is a lever at the left end of the carriage. It controls the amount of space between typed lines.

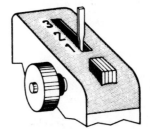

Fig. 2. Line-space regulator at "1"

   B. The line-space regulator has a 1, a 2, and a 3 printed beside it. Set it at:

   1 for single spacing, which leaves no blank lines between typed lines.

   2 for double spacing, which leaves one blank line between typed lines.

   3 for triple spacing, which leaves two blank lines between typed lines.

   EXAMPLES:

   ```
   Single Spacing    Double Spacing   Triple Spacing
   Single Spacing
   Single Spacing    Double Spacing
   Single Spacing                     Triple Spacing
   ```

3. **Set the Margin Stops Indicated at the Top of Each Lesson.**

   A. Your machine has a left margin stop and a right margin stop. Set them one at a time—first the left, then the right. The margin stops show where the typing line begins and ends.

   B. The procedure for setting the margin stops varies with the make and model of the machine. See the instruction booklet that comes with your machine, or ask your teacher.

Address on Letter and Envelope	Salutation and Complimentary Close
(18) *Mayor* Honorable (full name) Mayor of (City) City, State	Dear Mayor (last name): Sincerely yours,
(19) *President of a College or University* President (full name) Name of Institution City, State	Dear President (last name): Sincerely yours,
(20) *Professor in a college or University* Professor (full name) Name of Institution City, State	Dear Professor (last name): Sincerely yours,
(21) *Protestant Clergyman* Reverend (full name) Street City, State	Dear Reverend (last name): Sincerely yours,
(22) *Roman Catholic Priest* Reverend (full name) Street City, State	Dear Reverend Father: Sincerely yours,
(23) *Rabbi* Rabbi (full name) Street City, State	Dear Rabbi: Sincerely yours,
(24) *General, U. S. Army* General (full name) Address of Station	Dear General (last name): Sincerely yours,
(25) *Captain, U. S. Navy* Captain (full name) Address of Station	Dear Captain (last name): Sincerely yours,

4. **Pull the Paper Bail Away From the Cylinder.**
   A. The paper bail is the rod, with 2 small rollers on it, that clamps the paper against the cylinder.
   B. Pull the paper bail toward you, or straight up, so it won't interfere with inserting the paper (Fig. 3).

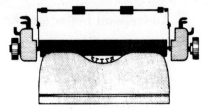

Fig. 3. Paper Bail Away from Cylinder

Use Standard Typing Paper 8½ by 11 in each lesson.

5. **Insert Your Paper.**
   A. Hold the paper in your left hand.
   B. Place it behind the cylinder against the paper guide.
   C. Turn the right cylinder knob to draw the paper into the machine. Turn up about half the length of the paper (Fig. 4).

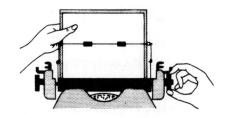

Fig. 4. Inserting the Paper

Fig. 5a. Straightening the Paper

6. **See Whether the Paper is Inserted Straight.**
   A. Your paper is inserted straight if the left edges—front and back—meet against the paper guide (Fig. 5a).
      If the edges do not meet—
   B. Loosen the paper: Depress the paper-release lever (Fig. 5b) at the right cylinder knob; then shift the paper till the left edges meet against the paper guide.
   C. Snap the paper release lever back to its normal position.

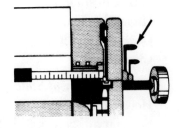

Fig. 5b. Paper Release Lever

Address on Letter and Envelope	Salutation and Complimentary Close
(9) *Representative* Honorable (full name) House of Representatives Washington, D. C. 20515	Dear Mr. (last name): Sincerely yours,
(10) *Librarian of Congress* Honorable (full name) Librarian of Congress Washington, D. C. 20540	Dear Mr. (last name): Sincerely yours,
(11) *Comptroller General* Honorable (full name) The Comptroller General of the United States Washington, D. C. 20548	Dear Mr. (last name): Sincerely yours,
(12) *The Chief of Justice* The Chief Justice The Supreme Court Washington, D. C. 20543	Dear Mr. Chief Justice: Sincerely yours,
(13) *Associate Justice* Mr. Justice (last name) The Supreme Court Washington, D. C. 20543	Dear Mr. Justice: Sincerely yours,
(14) *Judge of a Court* Honorable (full name) Judge of the (name of court) Street City, State	Dear Judge (last name): Sincerely yours,
(15) *Clerk of a Court* Mr. (full name) Clerk of the (name of court) Street City, State	Dear Mr. (last name): Sincerely yours,
(16) *Governor of a State* Honorable (full name) Governor of (State) City, State	Dear Governor (last name): Sincerely yours,
(17) *Secretary of State* (of a State) Honorable (full name) Secretary of State of (State) City, State	Dear Mr. Secretary: Sincerely yours,

7. **Leave a Top Margin of 1½ Inches.**
   A. Roll the paper down until its top edge is even with the aligning scale—on each side of the printing point (Fig. 6).
   B. Roll up 10 line spaces. All typewriters type 6 lines to the vertical inch (Fig. 7). By typing on line 10 from the top of the paper, you leave 9 blank lines—a top margin of 1½ inches.

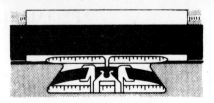

Fig. 6. Top edge of paper level with aligning scale

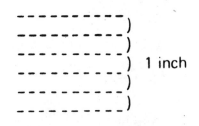

1 inch

Fig. 7. Six lines to the inch

8. **Set Paper Bail Back in Position.**
   A. Place the paper bail against the paper.
   B. Slide the small rollers on the bail to divide the paper approximately into thirds (Fig. 8).

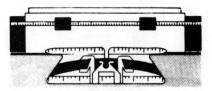

Fig. 8. Paper Bail Rollers in Place

SPECIAL FORMS OF ADDRESS, SALUTATION, AND COMPLIMENTARY CLOSE

Special forms of address, salutation, and complimentary close are used for people in high official positions and in special professions. The following forms are commonly used in addressing government officials, educators, clergymen, and members of the armed forces:

Address on Letter and Envelope	Salutation and Complimentary Close
(1) *The President* The President The White House Washington, D. C. 20500	Dear Mr. President: Respectfully yours,
(2) *The Vice President* The Vice President United States Senate Washington, D. C. 20510	Dear Mr. Vice President: Sincerely yours,
(3) *Member of Cabinet* The Honorable (full name) The Secretary of (Dept.) Washington, D. C.	Dear Mr. Secretary: Dear Madam Secretary: Sincerely yours,
(4) *Postmaster General* The Honorable (full name) The Postmaster General Washington, D. C. 20260	Dear Mr. Postmaster General: Sincerely yours,
(5) *The Attorney General* The Honorable (full name) The Attorney General Washington, D. C. 20530	Dear Mr. Attorney General: Sincerely yours,
(6) *American Ambassador* The Honorable (full name) American Ambassador City, Country	Sir: Very truly yours,
(7) *United States Senator* Honorable (full name) United States Senate Washington, D. C. 20510	Dear Senator(last name) Sincerely yours,
(8) *Speaker of the House of Representatives* Honorable (full name) Speaker of the House of Representatives Washington, D. C. 20510	Dear Mr. Speaker: Sincerely yours,

STEP 2: GET READY TO TYPE

1. Sit erect, directly in front of the machine, facing the book which should be at the right; hips back in the chair; feet flat on the floor; knees apart.

2. Lean forward from the waist up to about a handspan from the machine.

3. Relax your shoulders; let your arms and elbows hang loosely at your sides.

4. Place your fingertips *on the home keys:*
   Left fingertips on **A S D F**
   Right fingertips on: **J K L ;**

NOTE: **On Manual Machine**
   Curve all fingers deeply and rest them lightly on the keys.

   On Electric Machine
   Curve all fingers slightly and hold them as close to the keys as you can without quite touching them.

5. Keep wrists low, barely clearing the machine. Slant hands upward from the wrists parallel to the keyboard.

6. Curve left thumb close to first finger. Curve right thumb and hold it about 1/2 inch above the space bar, pointing to the letter B.

Good Typing Posture

Get Ready To Type

For Window Envelopes

1. Place the letter face up.

2. Bring the bottom edge up to about an inch below the inside address and crease.

3. Fold the exposed top part back along the line of the bottom edge and crease (Fig. 28).

4. Insert the letter in the envelope so that the inside address looks through the window (Fig. 29).

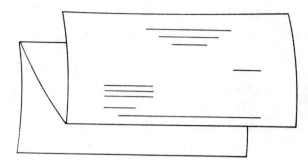

Fig. 28

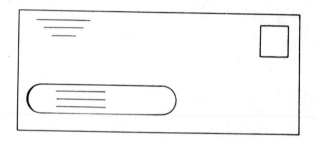

Fig. 29

Folding and Inserting a Letter

LESSON 1

HOME KEYS

<table>
<tr><td>A S D F</td><td>J K L ;</td></tr>
<tr><td>**Left hand**</td><td>**Right hand**</td></tr>
</table>

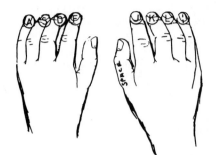

Note the difference between Pica and Elite type shown at the right. Compare this type with the type on your machine.

MARGINS: 15-70 (Pica)
25-80 (Elite)
SPACING: Single

```
This is Pica type: (10 spaces to the inch)
This is Elite type: (12 spaces to the inch)
```

How To Strike The Keys

Manual Machine: Strike each key firmly with your fingertip. Use short, sharp pecks. Release the key instantly—as if it were red hot. Fingers not typing stay close to their home keys.

Electric Machine: Tap each key lightly and quickly. Use a flat-oval motion. Hold your fingers above (not on) the keys. The keys on an electric machine respond instantly to very light strokes.

Follow each numbered step exactly.

1. **F-Key Tryout:** *Use Left First Finger*
Type the following **f**'s:

   ```
   ffffffffff
   ```

2. **J-Key Tryout:** *Use Right First Finger.*
Type the following **j**'s:

   ```
   ffffffffffjjjjjjjjjj
   ```

3. **Space Bar Tryout:** *Use Side of Right Thumb.*

   To leave a space after a letter or a word, strike the space bar sharply with the side of your right thumb.

   Type the following **f j** alternately. Space sharply after each letter. Bounce the thumb off the space bar.

   ```
   ffffffffffjjjjjjjjjj f j f j f j f j f j f j f j
   ```

FOLDING AND INSERTING A LETTER

For a Small Envelope: 3 Folds

1. Bring the bottom edge up to about ¼ inch from the top edge and crease (Fig. 21).

2. Bring the right edge toward the left about ⅓ the width of the paper and crease (Fig. 22).

3. Bring the left edge almost to the last fold and crease (Fig. 23).

4. Insert the folded letter:
   (a) Hold the envelope with reverse side facing you.
   (b) Insert the letter—last crease first (Fig. 24).

For a Large Envelope: 2 Folds

1. Bring bottom edge up to ⅓ the length of the paper and crease (Fig. 25).

2. Bring top edge down to almost the first crease, leaving a margin of about ¼ inch, and crease (Fig. 26).

3. Insert the folded letter:
   (a) Hold the envelope with reverse side facing you.
   (b) Insert the letter—last crease first (Fig. 27).

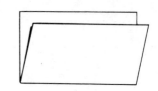

Fig. 21

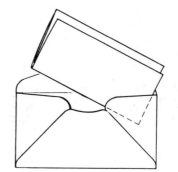

Fig. 22   Fig. 23

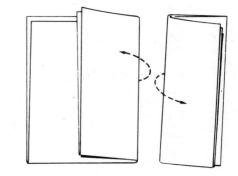

Fig. 24

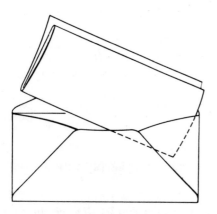

Fig. 27

Fig. 25

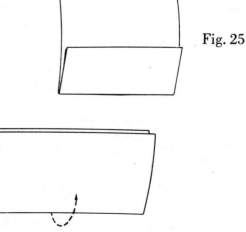

Fig. 26

4. Carriage-Return Practice:

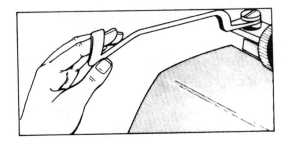

Fig. 9. Manual Machine

Fig. 10. Electric Machine

Manual Machine:

A. Swiftly move your left hand, fingers together and extended, to the carriage-return lever.

B. Flip the lever with a twist of the wrist, returning the carriage to the margin.

C. Zip your hand back home.

Electric Machine:

A. Swiftly extend the little finger of your right hand to the carriage-return key.

B. Lightly tap the return key, making the carriage return automatically to the margin.

C. Zip the finger back home.

Type the following line 5 times. Return the carriage without looking up.

fff jjj fff jjj fff jjj fff jjj fff jjj fff jjj fj

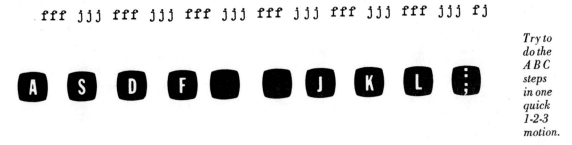

Try to do the A B C steps in one quick 1-2-3 motion.

5. **Home-Key Practice:** Type the following lines exactly. Double space after each 2-line group by using the carriage-return lever or carriage-return key twice. Doing so will leave one blank line between groups.

The Margin Bell tells you that you are getting close to the right margin stop.

FIRST FINGER:	fff jjj fff jjj fff jjj fff jjj fff jjj fff jjj fj fff jjj fff jjj fff jjj fff jjj fff jjj fff jjj fj
SECOND FINGER:	ddd kkk ddd kkk ddd kkk ddd kkk ddd kkk ddd kkk dk ddd kkk ddd kkk ddd kkk ddd kkk ddd kkk ddd kkk dk
THIRD FINGER:	sss lll sss lll sss lll sss lll sss lll sss lll sl sss lll sss lll sss lll sss lll sss lll sss lll sl
FOURTH FINGER:	aaa ;;; aaa ;;; aaa ;;; aaa ;;; aaa ;;; aaa ;;; a; aaa ;;; aaa ;;; aaa ;;; aaa ;;; aaa ;;; aaa ;;; a;

"Chainfeeding" Envelopes

"Chainfeeding" is a procedure that enables you to address a large number of envelopes quickly.

Fig. 20. Chain Feeding

1. Set the left margin stop at the desired point for the left margin of the address.

2. Insert envelope to typing position; then put a second envelope behind the cylinder.

3. Type the first envelope. Twirling it out draws the second one in; insert a third envelope behind the second. Twirling out the second envelope draws the third one in.

4. Continue the "chain." Have an envelope in back of the cylinder while you type the one in the machine.

Suggestion:

Learn to place the address by estimate—like business typists do. Note the amount of space to be left above the address. Practice twirling the envelope into the machine—without counting the lines from the top edge.

Typing Postal Cards

```
                    (1)        August 10, 1971

    (2) Dear Madam:

        The Philco TV set which you left with us for
    (3) repair is now ready for use.  We have checked (5)
        every part with extreme care and assure you
    (4) that it will now give perfect service.

        Please inform us when you will be at home to
        accept delivery.  The full charge is $23.75.

                            Sincerely yours,        (6)

                            APPLIANCE REPAIRS, INC. (7)
```

1. Date: On line 3 from top; start at about the center.
2. Salutation: On line 2 below the date.
3. Spacing: Single; one blank line between paragraphs.
4. Style: Blocked.
5. Margins: About ½ inch on each side.
6. Complimentary Close: On line 2 below last paragraph; start at about the center.
7. Firm Name: In CAPITALS, on line 2 below complimentary close.

   NOTE: Reference initials may be omitted.

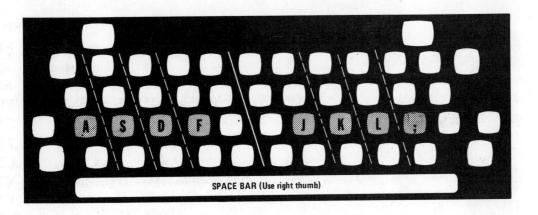

SPACE BAR (Use right thumb)

6. **Test Your Skill:** Type the following lines exactly. Double space after each 2-line group by using the carriage-return lever or the carriage-return key twice.

```
fff aaa ddd fad fad fad; jjj aaa lll jal jal jal;
fff aaa ddd fad fad fad; jjj aaa lll jal jal jal;

aaa lll aaa lll all all; ddd aaa ddd dad dad dad;
aaa lll aaa lll all all; ddd aaa ddd dad dad dad;

sss aaa ddd sad sad sad; aaa sss kkk ask ask ask;
sss aaa ddd sad sad sad; aaa sss kkk ask ask ask;
```
Space once after a semicolon.

```
a fad; ask dad; ask a lad; jal asks; a lad falls;
a fad; ask dad; ask a lad; jal asks; a lad falls;

all fads; alda asks; a sad lass; jal asks a lass;
all fads; alda asks; a sad lass; jal asks a lass;
```
All the home keys.

Use These New State Abbreviations
(All Capitals—Without Period)

Alabama	**AL**	Illinois	**IL**	Montana	**MT**	Puerto Rico	**PR**
Alaska	**AK**	Indiana	**IN**	Nebraska	**NB**	Rhode Island	**RI**
Arizona	**AZ**	Iowa	**IA**	Nevada	**NV**	South Carolina	**SC**
Arkansas	**AR**	Kansas	**KS**	New Hampshire	**NH**	South Dakota	**SD**
California	**CA**	Kentucky	**KY**	New Jersey	**NJ**	Tennessee	**TN**
Colorado	**CO**	Louisiana	**LA**	New Mexico	**NM**	Texas	**TX**
Connecticut	**CT**	Maine	**ME**	New York	**NY**	Utah	**UT**
Delaware	**DE**	Maryland	**MD**	North Carolina	**NC**	Vermont	**VT**
D. C.	**DC**	Massachusetts	**MA**	North Dakota	**ND**	Virginia	**VA**
Florida	**FL**	Michigan	**MI**	Ohio	**OH**	Washington	**WA**
Georgia	**GA**	Minnesota	**MN**	Oklahoma	**OK**	West Virginia	**WV**
Hawaii	**HI**	Mississippi	**MS**	Oregon	**OR**	Wisconsin	**WI**
Idaho	**ID**	Missouri	**MO**	Pennsylvania	**PA**	Wyoming	**WY**

Addressing Very Large Envelopes

To address an envelope too large for your typewriter—

1. Type the address on a label.
2. Paste the label in about the center of the envelope.

NOTE: If the envelope does not have the return address, type it in the upper left part of the label.

Fig. 11. Removing the paper

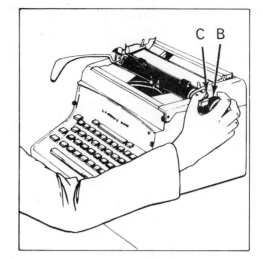

Fig. 12. Centering the carriage

Note: **WHEN YOU FINISH A LESSON**

A. Remove the paper: Depress paper release lever (A); gently pull out the paper; snap the lever back in place.

B. Center the carriage: Hold the right cylinder knob (B); press the carriage release lever (C); move the carriage to center of carriage scale; remove hand from lever.

C. Cover the typewriter.

D. If you are using an electric typewriter, turn the electric switch to OFF.

ADDRESSING ENVELOPES AND POSTAL CARDS

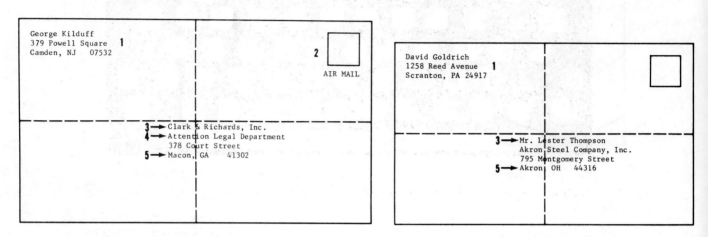

Standard Small envelope is $6\frac{1}{2}$ x $3\frac{5}{8}$ inches.
Standard Large envelope is $9\frac{1}{2}$ x $4\frac{1}{8}$ inches.

Standard Postal card is $5\frac{1}{2}$ x $3\frac{1}{4}$ inches.

The dotted lines show the vertical and horizontal centers.

The numbers in the illustrations are explained below:

1. Return Address:
   (If not printed)

   Block form, single space. Begin on line 3 from top edge and 3 spaces from left edge.

2. Mail Service:

   Type under the stamp any special notations such as AIR MAIL or REGISTERED.

3. Mailing Address:

   Envelopes and Postal Cards
   Block form, single space. Type the name at the estimated vertical center. This would be on line 12 of a small envelope, line 14 of a large envelope, line 10 of a postal card. Start it about $\frac{1}{2}$ inch to the left of the center point.

4. Special Notations:

   Type special notations such as Attention, Personal, Please Forward, under the name.

5. Zip Number:

   Type the zip number 3 spaces after the state. Use the new 2-letter state abbreviations listed on page 149, approved by the U.S. Postal Service.

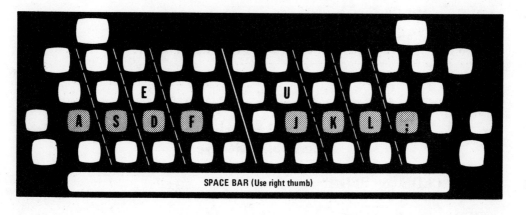

SPACE BAR (Use right thumb)

1. **Review:** Type each line twice. Double space after each 2-line group.

Always keep eyes on copy.

```
fff jjj ddd kkk sss lll aaa ;;; fdsa jkl; fdsajkl;
fad fad jal jal sad sad lad lad dad dad asks asks;
add add; dad dad; fall fall; asks asks; lass lass;
ask ada; ask jal; dad asks a lad; a sad lad falls;
ask a lad; jal asks a sad lad; a sad lad asks dad;
```

Think the finger and the key it controls.

2. **New-Key Practice: E**   *Use D-Finger.*

Practice the reach from **D** to **E** and back home to **D**. Keep the **A**-finger on its home key. When you can reach **E** without looking at your fingers, type each line twice:

Double space after each 2-line group.

```
e e e e ded ded ded ded; fed fed fed; led led led;
ded ded ded elk elk elk; jed jed jed; elf elf elf;
ded ded ded fee fee fee; see see see; ale ale ale;
ded ded ded lea lea lea; sea sea sea; eke eke eke;
fed led elk jed elf fee; see ale lea; sea jed eel;
```

Space once after a semicolon.

3. **New-Key Practice: U**   *Use J-Finger.*

Practice the reach from **J** to **U** and back home to **J**. Keep the **L** and **;** fingers on their home keys. When you can reach **U** without looking at your fingers, type each line twice:

```
u u u u juj juj juj juj; dud dud dud; due due due;
juj juj juj uke uke uke; use use use; sue sue sue;
juj juj juj jud jud jud; ula ula ula; auk auk auk;
juj juj juj flu flu flu; due due due; sud sud sud;
use dud due sud jud flu; eke auk ula; sue due use;
```

Return fingers quickly to home keys.

16. ABLE or IBLE?

A. Write *able* if you can form a word ending in *ation:*

   durable-duration; irritable-irritation

B. Write *ible* if you can form a word ending in *ion, tion,* or *ive:*

   accessible-accession; collectible-collection;
   digestible-digestive

17. CEED, CEDE, or SEDE?

CEED is only in: exceed, proceed, succeed
SEDE is only in: supersede
CEDE is in all other words: concede, intercede, precede,
                              recede, secede

18. PLURAL OF NOUNS

A. In most nouns, form the plural by adding *s:*

   house-houses; teacher-teachers

B. In nouns ending in *s, sh, ch,* and *x,* add *es:*

   bus-busses; brush-brushes; watch-watches; box-boxes

19. PLURAL OF COMPOUND NOUNS

A. If the noun consists of one word, add *s:*   cupful-cupfuls
                                          spoonful-spoonfuls

B. If the noun consists of more than one word, add *s* to the principal word:

   mother-in-law   editor-in-chief
   mothers-in-law   editors-in-chief

20. PREFIXES and SUFFIXES ENDING in ll

Omit one *l* in joining to other words: all-altogether
                                       full-wonderful

SPACE BAR (Use right thumb)

4. **Boost Your Skill:**

A. Type each line 3 times.

B. Practice words that have errors.

C. Try for a PERFECT copy of both lines.

All the keys you know.

Type at a steady, even pace.

```
ask sue; a full fee; use a desk; see a jade flask;
feed jal a salad; sue sells flasks; ella asks sue;
```

10. FINAL O

To Form The Plural:

A. If the *o* is after a vowel, add *s:*   cameo-cameos
    radio-radios

B. If the *o* is after a consonant, add *s or es:*   piano-pianos
    tomato-tomatoes

11. FINAL Y

To Form The Plural:

A. If the *y* is after a vowel, add *s:*   railway-railways
    attorney-attorneys

B. If the *y* is after a consonant, change *y* to *i* and add *es:*
    vacancy-vacancies
    country-countries

NOTE: Write the *y* before *ing:*   testify-testifying
    accompany-accompanying

12. FINAL F and FE

To Form The Plural:

A. Add *s:* roof-roofs; chief-chiefs; giraffe-giraffes

OR:

B. Change the *f* to *v* and add *s* or *es:*

life-lives; knife-knives; thief-thieves

13. FINAL CE or SE?

When the noun and verb are similar:

A. Write *ce* in nouns: advice, device, prophecy

B. Write *se* in verbs: advise, devise, prophesy

14. QU COMBINATION

Always write *u* after *q:* acquit, banquet, question

15. US or OUS?

A. Write *us* in nouns: callus, fungus, phosphorus

B. Write *ous* in adjectives: callous, serious, tedious

LESSON 3
NEW KEYS
R   I

MARGINS: 15-70 (Pica)
        25-80 (Elite)
SPACING: Single

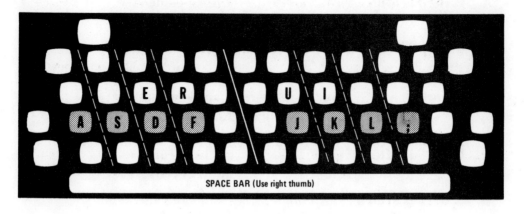

SPACE BAR (Use right thumb)

1. **Review:** Type each line twice. Double space after each 2-line group.

```
fff jjj ddd kkk sss lll aaa ;;; ded juj ded juj eu
ale elk jud use jake dues fuel fuse fake sulk jade
ask sue; a full fee; use a desk; see a jade flask;
a lad sees; a lad sees a duel; jud sells us seeds;
see us; sue sees us; use a desk; use a glass flask
```

Space quickly.

Keep elbows close to body.

2. **New-Key Practice: R**   *Use F-Finger.*
Practice the reach from **F** to **R** and back home to **F**. Keep the **A S D** fingers in home position. When you can reach **R** without looking at your fingers, type each line twice.

Return carriage without looking up.

```
r r r r frf frf frf frf; fur fur fur; jar jar jar;
frf frf frf are are are; ark ark ark; red red red;
frf frf frf rue rue rue; ear ear ear; ref ref ref;
frf frf frf era era era; ere ere ere; far far far;
red ark fur rue jar ref ear raj era are ruse lurk;
```

Type the first copy of each line slowly; then a little faster on the second.

3. **New-Key Practice: I**   *Use K-Finger.*
Practice the reach from **K** to **I** and back home to **K**. Keep semicolon-finger in home position. When you can reach **I** without looking at your fingers, type each line twice.

```
i i i i kik kik kik kik; irk irk irk; sir sir sir;
kik kik kik kid kid kid; air air air; fir fir fir;
kik kik kik rid rid rid; ail ail ail; lid lid lid;
kik kik kik die die die; aid aid aid; lie lie lie;
air fir kid sir rid rue lid lie aid ail sail jail;
```

Remember: Double space after each 2-line group.

4. **FINAL E**

   A. Write the final *e* before a suffix beginning with a consonant:

   hope-hopeful; care-careless; manage-management

   EXCEPTIONS: awe-awful; due-duly; whole-wholly; judge-judgment; argue-argument; acknowledge-acknowledgment

   B. Drop the final *e* before a suffix beginning with a vowel:

   admire-admirable; desire-desirable; please-pleasure

   EXCEPTIONS: notice-noticeable; change-changeable dye-dyeing; singe-singeing

5. **FINAL C**

   Add *k* before joining to *ed, er, ing,* or *y:*

   picnic-picnicked-picnicker-picnicking
   panic-panicky

6. **FINAL CE**

   Write the *e* before *able:*   peace-peaceable
                                     service-serviceable

7. **FINAL GE**

   Write the *e* before *ous:*   courage-courageous
                                     outrage-outrageous

8. **FINAL OE**

   Write the *e* before a suffix beginning with any vowel except *e:*

   hoe-hoeing-hoed
   toe-toeing-toed

9. **FINAL N**

   Write the *n* before *ness:*   mean-meanness
                                     sudden-suddenness

SPACE BAR (Use right thumb)

4. **Boost Your Skill:**
   A. Type each line 3 times.
   B. Practice words that have errors.
   C. Try for a PERFECT copy of both lines.

```
all is fair; sell us jars; a kid used a real idea;
fill a jar; fill a red jar; fill all red jars full
```
All the keys you know.

The following rules, without all the exceptions, provide a general guide to correct spelling and are adequate in most cases. When in doubt, use a good dictionary.

1. ADDING PREFIXES AND SUFFIXES

   A. A prefix is one or more letters added to the beginning of a word to change its meaning:

   il + legal = illegal   un + noticed = unnoticed
   im + mortal = immortal   dis + approve = disapprove

   B. A suffix is one or more letters added to the end of a word to change its meaning:

   sing + er = singer   pay + able = payable
   usual + ly = usually   heat + ing = heating

   C. Words may be divided at the end of a line between the prefix and the root and between the root and the suffix.

2. DOUBLING FINAL CONSONANTS

   A. In words of one syllable ending in a vowel and a consonant (except h or x), double the final consonant before ed, er, est, ing:

   plan   planned   planner   planning
   hot   hotter   hottest

   B. In words of more than one syllable ending in a vowel and a consonant and accented on the last syllable, follow the same rule as for words of one syllable: Double the final consonant before ed, er, est, ing:

   control   controlled   conroller   controlling   controllable
   regret   regretted   regretting   regrettable

3. EI or IE?

   A. Write ei after c when the sound is ee: deceit, deceive, ceiling, conceive, perceive, receive, receipt

   B. Write ie after other letters: belief, believe, chief, fiend, grief, mischief, pierce, relieve, reprieve, shriek, sieve

   EXCEPTIONS: counterfeit, forfeit, foreign, freight, height, leisure, neither, neighbor, seize vein, veil, weigh, weird

NEW KEYS
G O

MARGINS: 15-70 (Pica)
25-80 (Elite)
SPACING: Single

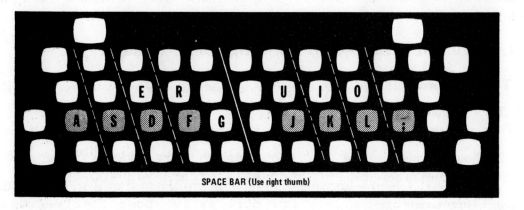

SPACE BAR (Use right thumb)

1. **Review:** Type each line twice. Double space after each 2-line group.

```
frf juj ded kik sss lll aaa ;;; frf juj ded kik ri
sir rue lid due ail jar kid ire fur auk jerk raid;
all is fair; sell us jars; a kid used a real idea;
russ is ill; fred uses skill; jed said alf is safe
all kids; all kids like; all kids sure like sleds;
```

Strike space bar sharply.

2. **New-Key Practice: G**   *Use F-Finger.*
Practice the reach from **F** to **G** and back home to **F**. Keep the **A S D** fingers in home position. When you can reach **G** without looking at your fingers, type each line twice:

```
g g g g fgf fgf fgf fgf; jug jug jug; rug rug rug;
fgf fgf fgf dig dig dig; leg leg leg; fig fig fig;
fgf fgf fgf sag sag sag; dug dug dug; gag gag gag;
rig rig rig egg egg egg; jig jig jig; keg keg keg;
jug jig rug fig age lug jag gas keg rag flag glad;
```

Zip fingers back to home keys.

3. **New-Key Practice: O**   *Use L-Finger.*
Practice the reach from **L** to **O** and back home to **L**. Keep the **J**-finger in home position. When you can reach **O** without looking at your fingers, type each line twice:

```
o o o o lol lol lol lol; old old old; oaf oaf oaf;
lol lol lol dog dog dog; oak oak oak; oar oar oar;
lol lol lol sol sol sol; jog jog jog; roe roe roe;
log log log joe joe joe; oil oil oil; our our our;
oil old dog jog sol log doe roe oaf foe golf goal;
```

RULES FOR TYPING NUMBERS (continued)

Type in Words:

1. A number that begins a sentence:

   Seventy boys entered the contest.

2. Round numbers, except when used in advertising:

   About one hundred men were there.
   Our sale offers you 100 bargains.

3. Approximate ages:

   Dr. Hartley is about thirty-five.

4. Isolated numbers ten and lower:

   Sidney lived ten years in Berlin.

5. Numbers ten and lower used as street names *except* with East, West, North, South:

   Martin lives at 490 Tenth Avenue.

   Fay lives at 87 West 10th Street.

6. Numbers used as proper names:

   David is in the Twelfth Regiment.

7. Indefinite sums of money:

   Al needs several hundred dollars.

8. Fractions standing alone:

   Mark ran three fourths of a mile.

9. Numbers 10 and lower, *except* when used with numbers above 10:

   We need 25 books on English; 9 on Mathematics; 7 on Economics; 8 on French; 4 on Drawing; 3 on Latin.

10. Time of day used informally:

    I saw Jim at a quarter past four.

    Time of day used with o'clock:

    Meet me at seven o'clock tonight.

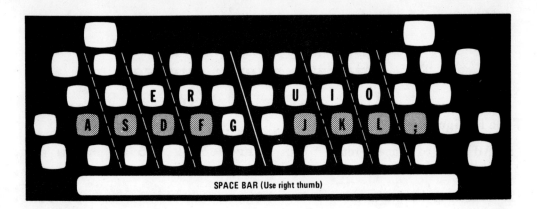

SPACE BAR (Use right thumb)

4. **Boost Your Skill:**
   A. Type each line 3 times.
   B. Practice words that have errors.
   C. Try for a PERFECT copy of both lines.

gail uses jugs; gail uses old jugs for salad oils;   *All the keys*
joe seeks four dark jade rugs for four glad girls;   *you know.*

RULES FOR TYPING NUMBERS

Type in Figures:

1. All sums of money—round numbers without ciphers:

   Max borrowed $2,175 to buy a car.
   Her ballpoint pen costs 98 cents.

2. Percentages and decimals:

   The highest rate was 4.8 percent.

3. Numbers with the symbols % # $:

   Cy's bonus of 5% amounts to $300.
   Rush order #69 for 75# of coffee.

4. Numbers after nouns:

   Act 4; Scene 2; Track 6; Room 12.

5. House numbers, except house number One

   Paul moved to 325 Stanton Street.
   Walt moved to One Delaney Street.

6. Measures, weights, distances, degrees, dimensions:

   10 quarts; 125 pounds; 650 miles.
   The temperature is 8° Fahrenheit.
   Our living room is 14 by 25 feet.

7. Numbers above ten:

   We ordered 11 more Spanish books.

8. Order, Invoice, Policy, Serial numbers—all without commas:

   Order No. 1623; Invoice No. 4958;
   Policy No. 5670; Serial No. 2079.

9. Numbers above TEN used as street names. Endings *th, nd, st,* may be omitted:

   Ben lives at 50 West 11th Street.
   Ralph lives at 39-68 52nd Avenue.
   Josephine lives at 472 91st Road.

10. Numbers and fractions in a series:

    Ship 5 bags, 10 boxes, 15 crates.
    1/2, 2/3, 3/4, 1/9, 2 5/6, 10 3/5

11. Time used with a.m. and p.m.:

    We plan to arrive home at 10 p.m.

12. The larger of two numbers used together:

    Robert needs 50 five-cent stamps.

13. Exact age in years, months, days:

    15 years, 10 months, 17 days old.

14. Graduation and historical dates:

    The class of '57. Spirit of '76.

15. Decades and centuries:

    The gay 1890's. The 9th century.

LESSON 5

NEW KEYS
Shift Keys . (Period)

MARGINS: 15-70 (Pica)
25-80 (Elite)

SPACING: Single

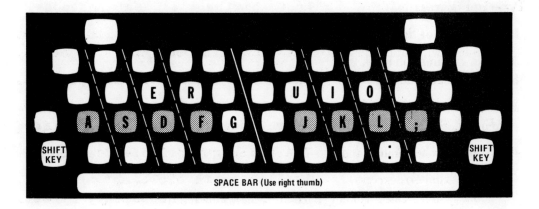

SPACE BAR (Use right thumb)

1. **Review:** Type each line twice. Double space after each 2-line group.

All the keys you know.

```
fdsa jkl; fdsa jkl; ask lad jal fad sad fall flask
frf juj ded kik fgf lol rig due old jugs kegs rode
all is fair; sell us jars; a kid used a real idea;
gail uses jugs; gail uses old jugs for salad oils;
joe seeks four dark jade rugs for four glad girls;
```

Keep your wrists as motionless as possible. Let your fingers do the work.

2. **New-Key Practice: Left Shift Key.** *Use A-Finger.*
To capitalize a letter typed by your right hand:
(1) Stretch **A**-finger to shift key, keeping **F**-finger at home.
(2) Hold shift key down while you type letter to be capitalized.
(3) Release shift key—zip fingers to home keys.

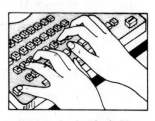

Fig. 13 Left Shift Key.

Type each line twice:

```
J J Ja Ja Jal Jal Jal; K K Ki Ki Kid Kid Kid;
L L Lo Lo Lou Lou Lou; U U Ul Ul Ula Ula Ula;
I I Id Id Ida Ida Ida; O O Ol Ol Ole Ole Ole;
```

Hold shift key down until you have struck and released the key for the capital letter.

RULES FOR PUNCTUATION SPACING

Space Once

1. After a comma: Mary is tall, blond, and pretty.

2. After a semicolon: You must study; or you may fail.

3. After an abbreviation: Prof. Smythe will lecture today.

4. Before and after the symbol **&**:   We bought it at Grove & Roberts.

5. After an exclamation mark within a sentence: Whew! how those jets zip across.

6. After a question mark within a sentence: Where are my books? my supplies?

7. Between a whole number and a "made" fraction: The red rug is 12 3/4 feet long. (BUT: The rug is 12½ feet long.)

Note: Do not space after the whole number if the fraction is on the keyboard.

Space Twice

8. After a sentence: I can do it. Can you? Show me.

9. After a colon: Our need: five new typewriters.
   Except when indicating time: Michael works from 8:30 to 4:30.

Do Not Space

10. Before or after an apostrophe: I borrowed my friend's overcoat.

11. Before or after a decimal point: Joe's savings amount to $629.50.

12. Between parentheses and the words they enclose: David Bowers (my pal) amuses me.

13. Between quotation marks and the words they enclose: Jack said, "I'll see you later."

14. Before or after a hyphen: My daughter-in-law is a teacher.

15. Before or after a dash: Vic wrote Fay--at my suggestion.

16. Before or after a comma in long numbers: We sold 2,980,745 yards of silk.

17. Before the symbol **%**:   Our 5% bonds fall due next week.

18. Between the symbol # and numerals: Order #93 was shipped yesterday. The package weighed exactly 26#.

19. After the period between small initials: The show starts at 8 p.m. sharp.

20. Before the symbols used for feet, inches, minutes, seconds: Mr. James Quincy is 5' 10" tall. Cal can run 850 yards in 1' 58".

Rules for Punctuation Spacing

3. **New-Key Practice: Right Shift Key.** *Use ;-Finger.*

To capitalize a letter typed by your left hand:
(1) Stretch **;**-finger to shift key, keeping **J**-finger at home.
(2) Hold shift key down while you type letter to be capitalized.
(3) Release shift key—zip fingers to home keys.

Fig. 14 Right Shift Key.

Type each line twice:

```
F F Fa Fa Fae Fae Fae;  G G Gu Gu Gus Gus Gus;    Depress
D D De De Del Del Del;  S S Sa Sa Sal Sal Sal;    shift key
A A Al Al Alf Alf Alf;  R R Ro Ro Rod Rod Rod;    firmly.
```

4. **New-Key Practice: . (Period)** *Use L-Finger.*

Practice the reach from **L** to Period and back home to **L**. Curl the **L**-finger as it goes downward. Keep the **J**-finger in home position. When you can reach the period without out looking at your fingers, type each line twice:

Space once after the period in abbreviations.

Jr. for Junior
Sr. for Senior
Dr. for Doctor
Ed. for Editor
Fr. for French
Rd. for Road

```
. . . . l.l l.l l.l l.l  Jr.  Jr.  Jr.  Sr.  Sr.  Sr.
Dr. Dr. Dr. Ed. Ed. Ed.  Fr.  Fr.  Fr.  Rd.  Rd.  Rd.
```

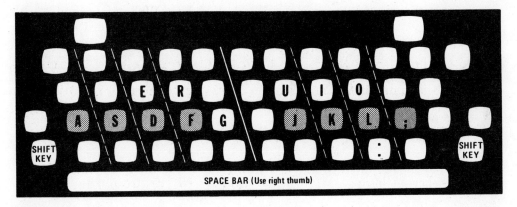

5. **Boost Your Skill:**
A. Type each line twice—smoothly.
B. Practice words that have errors.
C. Start over. See how many perfect pairs of lines you can turn out.

All the keys you know.

```
Joe fed us.  See Dr. Gold.  Lou asked for a salad.
Gus seeks oil.  Gus seeks a jug of oil for Gloria.
Lou sold all four dogs.  Jo said dogs fear a gale.
Ed uses a desk file.  A desk file is good for all.
All skills are good.  All skills are good if used.
```

Space twice after period at end of a sentence.

12. BUSINESS LETTERS

A. Address: Capitalize all titles in the address.

```
Mr. Harry Nevins, Manager
```

B. Salutation: Capitalize the first and last words, titles, and proper names in the salutation.

```
Dear Sir
My dear Sir
Dear Mr. Davis
```

C. Complimentary Close: Capitalize only the first word in the complimentary close.

```
Sincerely yours
Yours very truly
```

D. Closing Lines: Capitalize the title if it follows the name of the writer.

```
Thomas Ashton
President
```

MARGINS: 15-70 (Pica)
                25-80 (Elite)

SPACING: Single

1. **Review:** Type each line twice. Double space after each 2-line group.

```
fdsa jkl; fdsa jkl; ask sad lad jal fad fall flask
frf juj ded kik fgf lol rig due old jugs kegs rode
Flo Gus Del Sue Alf Rod Ella Joe Kid Lou Ole Ulaf;
Joe fed us.  See Dr. Gold.  Lou asked for a salad.
All skills are good.  All skills are good if used.
```

All the keys you know.

Return carriage without looking up.

2. **New-Key Practice: T** *Use F-Finger.*

Practice the reach from **F** to **T** and back home to **F**. Keep the **A** and **S** fingers in home position. When you can reach **T** without looking at your fingers, type each line twice:

```
t t t t ftf ftf ftf ftf; fit fit fit; lot lot lot;
ftf ftf ftf rut rut rut; jet jet jet; kit kit kit;
ftf ftf ftf tea tea tea; sit sit sit; tug tug tug;
toe toe toe dot dot dot; ate ate ate; jut jut jut;
fit lot rut jet kit tea sit tug dot jut true tire;
```

Eyes on copy. Be a touch typist.

3. **New-Key Practice: H** *Use J-Finger.*

Practice the reach from **J** to **H** and back home to **J**. Keep the **K L ;** fingers in home position. When you can reach **H** without looking at your fingers, type each line twice:

```
h h h h jhj jhj jhj jhj; hut hut hut; her her her;
jhj jhj jhj hat hat hat; had had had; she she she;
jhj jhj jhj hag hag hag; hoe hoe hoe; ash ash ash;
hue hue hue hit hit hit; hot hot hot; the the the;
hug hoe has hat hid she rush josh fish hook hills;
```

6. HISTORICAL DOCUMENTS, EVENTS, MONUMENTS

Capitalize historical documents, events, and monuments:

```
Declaration of Independence
Battle of Gettysburg
Statue of Liberty
```

7. SEASONS OF THE YEAR

Do not capitalize: spring ... summer ... autumn ... winter

8. GEOGRAPHICAL NAMES AND NAMES OF BUILDINGS

Capitalize geographical names and names of buildings:

```
East River
Atlantic Ocean
Rocky Mountains
Empire State Building
```

Do not capitalize east, west, north, south when used to indicate direction:

```
Drive north on Broadway, then turn west on
42nd Street.
```

9. COMPANIES, ORGANIZATIONS, INSTITUTIONS, GOVERNMENT AGENCIES

Capitalize the names of companies, organizations, institutions, and Government agencies:

```
Arco Publishing Company, Inc.
American Automobile Association
Columbia University
Federal Communications Commission
```

10. NOUNS

A. Capitalize a noun when it is part of a specific name:

```
Bentley School
```

B. Capitalize all proper nouns and their derivatives:

```
Mexico ...... Mexican
South ....... Southerner
Elizabeth ... Elizabethan
```

11. LANGUAGES, RELIGIONS, THE DEITY

Capitalize languages, religions, and words denoting the Deity:

```
Spanish
Mohammedan
God
```

4. **Boost Your Skill:**
   A. Type each line 3 times.
   B. Practice words that have errors.
   C. Try for a PERFECT copy of both lines.

To avoid Key Jams: Type evenly—one key at a time. Release it instantly.

```
Joel got to that lake at four.  He hooked a trout.
Ask Gil or Kurt to look for Hale at the old house.
```

5. **Figure Your Speed:** You can tell how fast you type by timing yourself, or by having someone time you.

   A. Note the word-count scale below. It shows that every 5 strokes—letters, punctuation marks, and spaces—count as 1 word. The scale shows that each of the 2 lines above it has 10 words.
   B. If you type the first line in 1 minute, your speed is 10 words a minute. If you type both lines in 1 minute, your speed is 2 x 10 = 20 words a minute.
   C. If you type part of a line, note the number above which you stopped; it tells you how many words to count for that part of the line.

   EXAMPLE: In a 1-minute timing, you typed the first line and had to stop after typing the word "right" in the second line. Your speed would be:

   > 10 words in line 1
   > 6 words in line 2
   >
   > 16 words in 1 minute

6. **Test Your Skill:** *Take Three 1-Minute Timings*

Follow these steps in all your 1-minute timings.

   A. Repeat if you finish before end of 1 minute.
   B. After each timing, jot down total words typed and total errors. Count only one error in a word even if it has more.
   C. Practice the words that have errors till they are easy for you.
   D. Record on your 1-Minute Score Sheet (page 159) your best speed within 3 errors. Goal: 15 words a minute within 3 errors.

WORDS

All the keys you know.

```
Jill has a silk skirt.  Her sister got it for her.     10
The skirt fits her just right.  Dora likes it too.     20
....1....2....3....4....5....6....7....8....9....10
```

RULES FOR CAPITALIZATION

1. **GENERAL RULE**

   A. Capitalize the first word of a complete sentence:

   ```
   Mr. Hale is our office manager.
   ```

   B. Capitalize the first word of a quoted sentence:

   ```
   He said, "Mr. Hale is our office manager."
   ```

   Note: Do not capitalize the first word of a quotation if it is not a complete sentence:

   ```
   He said that Mr. Hale is "our office manager."
   ```

   Do not capitalize the first word of a quotation that is resumed within a sentence:

   ```
   "I'll phone Joe," she said, "while you dress."
   ```

2. **AFTER A COLON**

   Capitalize the first word after a colon if that word begins a complete sentence:

   ```
   Here is Mr. Hale's message: Mail all the
   letters today.
   ```

3. **TITLES OF PERSONS**

   A. Capitalize a title when it applies to a specific person:

   ```
   President Nixon signed the welfare bill.
   ```

   B. Capitalize a title standing alone if it is of high distinction:

   ```
   The President vetoed the welfare bill.
   The Governor will speak to us tonight.
   ```

4. **TITLES OF PUBLICATIONS**
   (Books, Magazines, Newspapers, Articles, Plays, etc.)

   Capitalize the first word and every important word in the title:

   ```
   Sixty Years on the Firing Line   (book)
   Death of a Salesman              (play)
   ```

5. **DATES, MONTHS, HOLIDAYS**

   Capitalize the days of the week, months of the year, and holidays:

   ```
   Friday
   December
   Christmas
   ```

Rules for Capitalization

LESSON 7
NEW KEYS
W Y , (Comma)

MARGINS: 15-70 (Pica)
25-80 (Elite)

SPACING: Single

1. **Review:** Type each line twice. Double space after each 2-line group.

```
fgf jhj fdsa jkl; fgf jhj fdsa jkl; fgf jhj fg jh;
frf juj ftf jhj fgf kik ded lol ss aa l. l. l. l.l
jug led for ask sag hit jet out sol tug goes salt;
Jill has a silk skirt.  Her sister got it for her.
The skirt fits her just right.  Dora likes it too.
```

Return fingers quickly to home keys. Keep elbows close to body.

2. **New-Key Practice: W** *Use S-Finger.*
Practice the reach from **S** to **W** and back home to **S**. Keep the **F**-finger close to its home key. Try to hold elbow close to body. When you can reach **W** without looking at your fingers, type each line twice:

```
w w w w sws sws sws sws; sow sow sow; low low low;
sws sws sws was was was; few few few; row row row;
sws sws sws wag wag wag; how how how; jaw jaw jaw;
who who who wit wit wit; dew dew dew; awl awl awl;
dew row was law few wag how jaw wit wed work slow;
```

Type at a steady, even pace.

3. **New-Key Practice: Y** *Use J-Finger.*
Practice the reach from **J** to **Y** and back home to **J**. Keep the **K L ;** fingers in home position. When you can reach **Y** without looking at your fingers, type each line twice:

THE HYPHEN (continued)

8. Use a hyphen in compound nouns consisting of three or more words:

```
brother-in-law
teacher-in-charge
```

9. Use a hyphen in compound words beginning with **self**:

```
a self-explanatory letter
a self-addressed envelope
```

10. Use a hyphen in a series of hyphenated words having the same ending:

```
We get first-, second-, and third-class mail.
```

THE DASH

1. Use a dash to indicate an abrupt break in a sentence:

```
Mr. Pearson left--where did he go?
```

2. Use a dash for emphasis:

```
Type two hyphens--without spacing--for a dash.
```

3. Use a dash to set off a short, final summary:

```
She had only one pleasure--dancing.
```

4. Use a dash to indicate the name of an author after a direct quotation:

```
"To sin by silence when they should protest
makes cowards out of men."--Abraham Lincoln
```

5. Use a dash to set off an explanatory group of words:

```
His food--nuts, berries, fish--kept him alive.
```

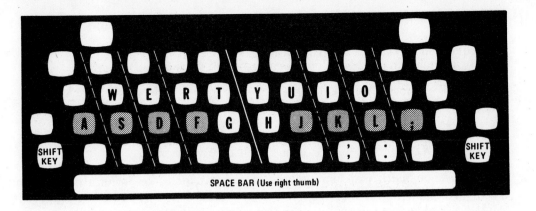

```
y y y y jyj jyj jyj jyj; yet yet yet; yak yak yak;
jyj jyj jyj shy shy shy; sly sly sly; way way way;
jyj jyj jyj try try try; why why why; dry dry dry;
yes yes yes jay jay jay; sly sly sly; fry fry fry;
guy say dye you key lay joy toy hay day eye yield;
```

Use finger-reach action only; arms and hands quiet.

4. **New-Key Practice: , (Comma)**   *Use K-Finger.*

Practice the reach from **K** to **,** and back home to **K**. Curl the **K**-finger as it goes downward. Keep the **;**-finger in home position. When you can reach the **,** without looking at your fingers, type each line twice:

All the keys you know.

```
, , , k,k k,k k,k yak, yak, yak; lark, lark, lark;
k,k k,k k,k work, work, work; sheik, sheik, sheik;
jerk, fork, dark, silk, lurk, stork, freak, Greek;
```

Space once after a comma and semicolon.

5. **Boost Your Skill:**
   A. Type each line 3 times—smoothly.
   B. Practice words that have errors.
   C. Try for a PERFECT copy of both lines.

```
Yes, Walt took the test.  He told Jud it was easy.
Take the ferry, Edward.  You will get there early.
```

All the keys you know.

6. **Test Your Skill:** *Take Three 1-Minute Timings.*

   Goal: 15 words a minute within 3 errors.

   Record your best speed within 3 errors.

WORDS

All the keys you know.

```
Try to do the work just right if you do it at all.   10
Good daily work is a sure way to get to your goal.   20
....1....2....3....4....5....6....7....8....9....10
```

Lesson 7: W Y , (Comma)

QUESTION MARK

1. Use a question mark after a direct question.

```
Do you know his address?
```

But: After a question which is in the form of a request, use a period.

```
May we have your check next week.
Will you please mail an estimate.
```

2. Use a question mark with parentheses to express doubt or uncertainty concerning a statement immediately preceding.

```
He was born May 10, 1892 (?).
```

EXCLAMATION POINT

Use an exclamation point to express strong feeling or emotion.

```
Welcome home, son!
Rush, it's urgent!
```

THE HYPHEN

1. Use a hyphen to divide a word at the end of a line. Make the division between syllables. Never type a hyphen at the beginning of a line.

2. Use a hyphen to join words serving as a single adjective *before* a noun:

```
He is a well-known writer.
```

3. Use a hyphen in spelling fractions serving as modifiers:

```
        The job is two-thirds done.
But: Two thirds of the job is done.
```

4. Use a hyphen in spelling the compound numbers twenty-one through ninety-nine.

5. Use a hyphen to form compound verbs:

```
Double-check every entry.
Do not side-step your duty.
```

6. Use a hyphen with **ex** and **elect**:

```
ex-President Johnson
Mayor-elect Lindsay
```

7. Use a hyphen to avoid a confusing union of letters:

```
re-enter
pro-ally
```

Rules for Puntuation

LESSON 8
NEW KEYS
Q P : (Colon)

MARGINS: 15-70 (Pica)
25-80 (Elite)
SPACING: Single

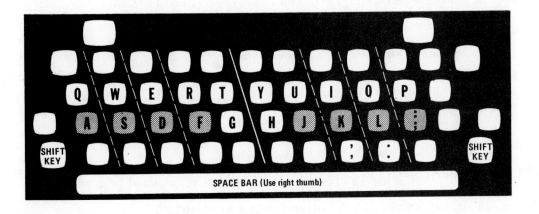

1. **Review:** Type each line twice. Double space after each 2-line group.

```
frf juj ftf jyj fgf jhj ded kik sws lol aaa ;;; wy
kit yet lid why fir how use sir tow jig lye aid so
The daily drills will aid you to get to your goal.
Yes, Flora; Judith does her task with great skill.
Walter told Jerry Hale that he hooked a huge fish.
```

Type smoothly— without pausing. Keep the carriage moving.

2. **New-Key Practice: Q** *Use A-Finger.*
Practice the reach from **A** to **Q** and back home to **A**. Keep the **F**-finger on its home key. Keep elbow close to your side. When you can reach **Q** without looking at your fingers, type each line twice:

```
q q q q aqa aqa aqa aqa; aqua aqua; quotes quotes;
aqa aqa aqa quit quit; quail quail; liquor liquor;
aqa aqa aqa quay quay; quite quite; quaffs quaffs;
aqa aqa aqa quid quid; quirk quirk; quires quires;
quit quid quad quest quote quite quilt quash quake
```

Sit straight. Keep wrists low without touching machine.

3. **New-Key Practice: P** *Use ;-Finger.*
Practice the reach from **;** to **P** and back home to **;**. Keep the **J K** fingers close to their home keys. Keep elbow close to your side. When you can reach **P** without looking at your fingers, type each line twice:

THE APOSTROPHE (continued)

(d) In compound words, add 's:

    father-in-law's car

(e) In joint ownership, add 's to last name only:

    Sue and Laura's room

(f) In separate ownership, add 's to each name:

    Sue's and Laura's rooms

(g) In indefinite pronouns, add 's:

    one's best efforts
    each other's rights

NOTE: Do not use an apostrophe with possessive personal pronouns:

    his, hers, its, ours, yours, theirs

2. Use an apostrophe to indicate a contraction:

    isn't (is not)
    wasn't (was not)

3. Use an apostrophe to indicate feet and minutes after figures:

    Hy made the mile in 5'.
    The block is 125' long.

4. Use an apostrophe to indicate the omission of numbers:

    the spirit of '76

5. Use an apostrophe to indicate plurals of figures and letters:

    5's
    A's

PARENTHESES

1. Use parentheses to enclose explanatory or added information.

    In our office (and in most offices) the
    Blocked Style of business letter is used.

2. Use parentheses to enclose enumerated items:

    Employers seek workers who are (1) accurate,
    (2) dependable, and (3) productive.

3. Use parentheses to enclose figures after amounts that are spelled out.

    The monthly rent is two hundred dollars ($200).

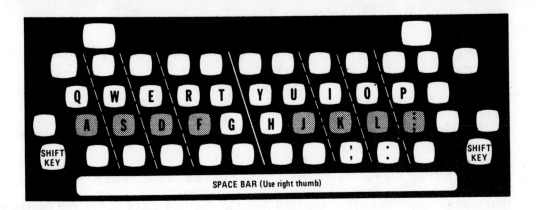

```
p p p p  ;p;  ;p;  ;p;  ;p;  pal pal pal;  pit pit pits;
;p;  ;p;  ;p;  pay pay pay;  par par par;  pie pie pie;
;p;  ;p;  ;p;  put put put;  pig pig pig;  paw paw paw;
pep pep pep sip sip sip;  hip hip hip;  fop fop fop;
lip fop sap hip gyp dip put kip paw rip jeep quip;
```
Keep right thumb curved, close to the space bar.

4. **New-Key Practice: Colon.**   *Use ;-Finger.*
To type the colon, depress the left shift key and strike the ;-key.

Space twice after a colon,
except when indicating time.

EXAMPLES:
```
Foods we need:  butter, eggs, milk.
His working hours are 8:30 to 4:15.
```

Type each line twice:

```
: : : ;:; ;:; ;:; Dear Gay:  Dear Pal:  Dear Kurt:
Dear Joe:  Walt stayed at Hotel Quill till Friday.
```
All the keys you know.

5. **Boost Your Skill:**
   A. Type each line 3 times—smoothly.
   B. Practice words that have errors.
   C. Try for a PERFECT copy of both lines.

Space once after period following a capital initial.

```
Judge Paul K. Quale did free the slow, tired jury.
Joe Yale will take Paula Quat to the party Friday.
```

6. **Test Your Skill:** *Take Three 1-Minute Timings.*
   Goal: 15 words a minute within 3 errors.
   Record your best speed within 3 errors.

WORDS

All the keys you know.
```
Dear Joe:  Gus Quill says he types all the letters      10
for his father.  This work surely tests his skill.      20
....1....2....3....4....5....6....7....8....9....10
```

Lesson 8: Q P : (Colon)   27

QUOTATION MARKS (continued)

6. In a long quotation, use quotation marks only at the beginning of each paragraph and at the end of the last paragraph.

7. WITH QUESTION MARK

   A. If the entire sentence is a question, put the question mark outside the quotation marks:

   ```
   Did Harry say, "I have just mailed the letter"?
   ```

   B. If only the quotation is a question, put the question mark inside the quotation marks:

   ```
   Mr. Farley inquired, "Has the manager arrived?"
   ```

8. WITH EXCLAMATION MARK

   A. If the entire sentence is an exclamation, put the exclamation mark outside the quotation marks:

   ```
   How foolish it is for the neighbors to "argue"!
   ```

   B. If only the quotation is an exclamation, put the exclamation mark inside the quotation marks:

   ```
   Ken Riley shouted, "Dave hit another home run!"
   ```

THE APOSTROPHE

1. Use an apostrophe to show possession:

   (a) In singular and plural nouns not ending in s, add 's:

   ```
   boy's shoes
   men's coats
   ```

   (b) In singular nouns ending in s, add an apostrophe only:

   ```
   Dickens' novels
   Charles' papers
   ```

   OR add 's _____ Dickens's novels
   Charles's papers

   THE SECOND FORM SEEMS PREFERRED. BOTH ARE CORRECT.

   (c) In plural nouns ending in s, add apostrophe only:

   ```
   lawyers' offices
   ```

   NOTE: In plural company and organization names that are possessive, omit the apostrophe:

   ```
   Teachers College
   Bankers Trust Co.
   ```

Rules for Puntuation

LESSON 9
THE TABULATOR

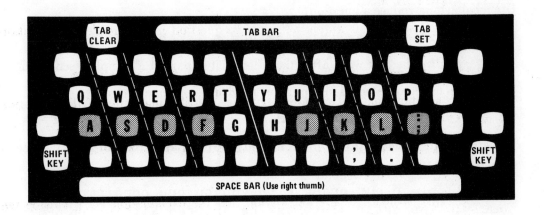

1. **Review:** Type each line twice. Double space after each 2-line group.

```
frf juj ftf jyj fgf jhj ded kik sws lol aqa ;p; gh
fish joke girl quit tops glad warp quay work equal
If Lee Quag types the work, he does it just right.
Haste is waste.  Take it easy.  Life is too short.
Dear Jo:  Kate says it is quite easy to type well.
```

All the keys you know. Start each new line quickly.

2. **The Tabulator:** Your typewriter has a Tabulator—a device that makes the carriage hop to any scale point you desire. The Tabulator has three parts: a CLEAR key, a SET key, and a TAB key, or bar. To adjust your machine for indenting, follow these steps:

(1) Clear the machine: Remove any stops that may already be set. (A) Move carriage to right margin stop; (B) hold down the CLEAR KEY while returning carriage to left margin stop.

(2) Set desired tab stops: Space across the paper and press SET KEY once, firmly, at each desired stopping point.

(3) Draw carriage back to left margin.

(4) Tabulate: Hop the carriage to each tab stop. On Manual Machine, hold down firmly the TAB KEY or TAB BAR till carriage stops. Use the little finger on the TAB KEY, the right first finger on the TAB BAR (Fig. 15-16—next page.)

On Electric Machine, flick the TAB KEY lightly with the little finger and zip the finger back home.

THE COLON

1. Use a colon to introduce a listing:

   ```
   I bought these items: a tie, a shirt, and a hat.
   ```

2. Use a colon to introduce a question:

   ```
   What I wish to know is:  Are you a touch typist?
   ```

   Note: Capitalize the first word after the colon if it is part of a complete sentence.

3. Use a colon to separate hours and minutes in expressing time:

   ```
   We arrived home at 2:30 a.m.
   ```

4. Use a colon after such expressions as **namely, for example, as follows**, if a series or a statement follows:

   ```
   We shall place our order with you on one condition,
   namely:  The entire lot must be shipped within ten
   days after receipt of the order.
   ```

5. Use a colon after the salutation in business letters:

   ```
   Dear Sir:
   Dear Mr. Smith:
   Gentlemen:
   ```

QUOTATION MARKS

1. Use quotation marks to enclose titles of articles, plays, poems, essays, lectures, and the like:

   ```
   I have read the article "Campus Revolution."
   ```

2. Use quotation marks to enclose direct quotations:

   ```
   Emerson said, "The only way to have a
   friend is to be one."
   ```

3. Use quotation marks to enclose each separate speech:

   ```
   "I am sure," he said, "that we have met before."
   ```

   Rule: Put the comma and period inside quotation marks.

4. Use quotation marks to enclose special words—for emphasis:

   ```
   I will check "debit"; you will check "credit."
   Our company's "slogan":  QUALITY FIRST--ALWAYS
   ```

   Rule: Put the semicolon and colon outside quotation marks.

5. Use an apostrophe to enclose a quotation within a quotation:

   ```
   Thomas said, "The command 'Don't give up
   the ship' was given by John Paul Jones."
   ```

Rules for Punctuation

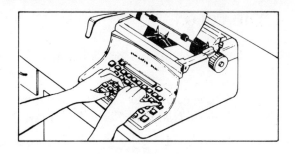

Fig. 15. Using the Tab Bar

Fig. 16. Using the
Tab Key

3. **Tabulating Practice:**
   A. Clear the machine.
   B. Set tab stops: Pica Type .... at 30, 45, and 60
                    Elite Type .... at 40, 55, and 70
   C. Type the columns horizontally—across the paper.
      Tabulate: Use the Tab Key or Tab Bar to hop the carriage to columns 2, 3, and 4.

   Note: Column 1 begins at your left margin.

Margin ↓	*Tab Stop* ↓	*Tab Stop* ↓	*Tab Stop* ↓
quip	keep	used	park
high	quit	goes	jolt
daft	eyes	stay	with
sure	jury	feed	drew
your	list	sail	work

All the keys you know.

Reach for the tab key or bar without looking up.

4. **Paragraph Typing:**
   A. Paragraphs may be single-spaced or double-spaced.
   B. When paragraphs are single-spaced, the first word may begin at the margin—as in Example 1. Or it may be indented 5 spaces—as in Example 2.
   C. When paragraphs are double-spaced, the FIRST word MUST be indented 5 spaces —as in Example 3 —next page.
   D. All paragraphs—single- or double-spaced—MUST be separated by one blank line.

EXAMPLE 1: *Single-spaced, blocked*

```
Correct typing posture
is much more important
than you think.

It helps to build your
skill at a much faster
rate than poor posture.
```

EXAMPLE 2: *Single-spaced, indented*

```
    Correct typing posture
is much more important than
you think.

    It helps to build your
skill at a much faster rate
than poor posture.
```

THE COMMA (continued)

8. Use a comma to separate thousands, millions, billions—except in Order Numbers, Invoice Numbers, Serial Numbers, Policy Numbers:

   3,791   25,132   4,392,690   2,365,930,038

9. Use a comma between title and name of organization if **of** or **of the** has been omitted:

   ```
   President, New York University
   Superintendent, Board of Education
   ```

10. Use a comma before **and, but, for, or, neither, nor**—when it joins two main clauses:

   ```
   Many are called, but few are chosen.
   Ted shaved quickly, for he was late.
   ```

THE SEMICOLON

1. Use a semicolon between clauses not joined by a connective:

   ```
   We may not go after all; we may stay home.
   ```

2. Use a semicolon between clauses joined by such connectives as **therefore, however, otherwise, nevertheless**:

   ```
   Mr. Roe is very well-known here; nevertheless, we cannot
   extend unlimited credit to him.
   ```

   Note: Use a comma after the connective.

3. Use a semicolon to separate a series of phrases or clauses that contain commas:

   ```
   The boys enjoyed their vacation in many ways; in the
   morning, by fishing; in the afternoon, by playing
   tennis; and in the evening, by indoor games.
   ```

4. Use a semicolon before such introductory expressions as **for example, namely, such as**:

   ```
   You need to do much research before you can write
   the speech; for example, you must read some books
   on the subject.
   ```

5. Use a semicolon to connect two short related sentences:

   ```
   Let's camp here; there's a lake nearby.
   ```

Rules for Punctuation

```
      Correct typing posture

   is much more important than

   you think.

      It helps to build your

   skill at a much faster rate

   than poor posture.
```

5. **Paragraph Practice:** Double Spaced
   You get one extra word credit each time you use the Tab Bar or Tab Key.
   A. Clear the machine.
   B. Set a tab stop 5 spaces from left margin.
   C. Set line-space regulator at "2" for double spacing. Double spacing shows 1 blank line between typed lines.
   D. Type each paragraph slowly, smoothly. Practice each word that has an error. Try for a PERFECT copy of each paragraph.

WORDS

```
   Your goal is good skill.  The way to get good      10

skill is to work hard for it.  It is the sure way.    20
....1....2....3....4....5....6....7....8....9....10
```
All the keys you know.
```
   So quit the talk.  Just work for the goal you       10

seek.  Put forth good effort.  Reward will follow.    20
....1....2....3....4....5....6....7....8....9....10
```

6. **Test Your Skill:** *Take Three 1-Minute Timings.*
   Goal: 15 words a minute within 3 errors.
   Record your best speed within 3 errors.

Single-Spaced, Blocked Paragraph.
Set Line-Space Regulator at "1."

All the keys you know.
```
Dear Walt:  Go with Joel Qualey to see if that old    10
house at the edge of the park lake is still there.    20
....1....2....3....4....5....6....7....8....9....10
```

Lesson 9: The Tabulator

RULES FOR PUNCTUATION

THE PERIOD

1. Use a period after a statement:

   The material will be shipped today.

2. Use a period after an abbreviation:

   Mr. Bradley is moving to St. Louis.

3. Use a period for a decimal point in numbers:

   Our overtime rate is $4.50 an hour.

4. Use a period after each initial in a person's name:

   Mr. E. S. Goldman will call on you.

THE COMMA

1. Use a comma to separate words, phrases, or clauses in a series:

   The display consists of rings, watches, and bracelets.
   Mary will shop for you, cook for you, and sew for you.

2. Use a comma after an introductory word, phrase, or clause:

   However, I am inclined to agree with you.
   In the meantime, we have decided to wait.
   After I endorsed the check, he mailed it.

3. Use a comma to set off a word, phrase, or clause that is not essential to the thought in a sentence:

   Our manager, Mr. Ralph Dix, is on vacation.
   Her mother, who is in Paris, telephoned me.

4. Use a comma to set off words in direct address:

   Will you, Mr. Hampton, write the letter?

5. Use a comma before short direct quotations:

   He said, "I am leaving for London tomorrow."

6. Use a comma to indicate the omission of a word:

   Henry is tall; Walter, short.

7. Use a comma to separate two words or figures that may be confusing:

   To Robert, Thomas was a perfect gentleman.
   In 1941, 30 ships were lost in one day.
   Instead of 25, 52 men applied for the job.

LESSON 10
NEW KEYS
C V / (SLANT)

Margins: 15-70 (Pica)
25-80 (Elite)
Spacing: Single

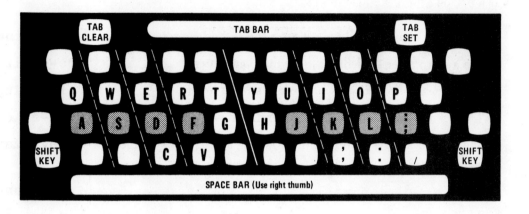

1. **Review:** Type each line twice. Double space after each 2-line group.

```
frf juj ftf jyj fgf jhj ded kik sws lol aqa ;p; qp
word fish joke quay girl harp quit glad tops equal
Look at your work; it tells you how well you type.
We will offer all help to the quiet lad who works.
Judge Kurt P. Quays will free the slow jury today.
```

All the keys you know.

Space quickly after each word.

2. **New-Key Practice: C** *Use D-Finger.*

Practice the reach from **D** to **C** and back home to **D**. Curl the **D**-finger as it reaches down to **C**. Keep the **A**-finger in home position. When you can reach **C** without looking at your fingers, type each line twice:

```
c c c c dcd dcd dcd dcd; cut cut cut; cue cue cue;
dcd dcd dcd cur cur cur; cud cud cud; cup cup cup;
dcd dcd dcd cat cat cat; cap cap cap; cow cow cow;
dcd dcd dcd cod cod cod; ice ice ice; cog cog cog;
cut cap cog cry cod cow cash jack calf tack quick;
```

In the word ice, line 4, zip D-finger from C to E without pausing on home key.

3. **New-Key Practice: V** *Use F-Finger.*

Practice the reach from **F** to **V** and back home to **F**. Keep the **A S D** fingers in home position. When you can reach **V** without looking at your fingers, type each line twice:

```
v v v v fvf fvf fvf fvf; via via via; vow vow vow;
fvf fvf fvf vet vet vet; vie vie vie; eve eve eve;
fvf fvf fvf Vic Vic Vic; Val Val Val; vat vat vat;
pave pave pave; void void void; Vicki Vicki Vicki;
rave vows jive gave have five caves quiver voyage;
```

RULES FOR WORD DIVISION

1. Divide a word only between syllables .... `con-sist`

2. Divide a word between double consonants .... `mat-ter`

   Note: If a word is derived from a word already ending in a double consonant, divide it after the second consonant .... `add-ing`

3. Divide a word after a prefix of more than one letter .... `pre-scribe`

4. Divide a word before a suffix of more than one letter .... `lead-ing`

5. Divide a word between two vowels coming together .... `gradu-ation`

6. Divide a word after a vowel—if the vowel is a separate syllable `regu-lar`

7. Divide a word between two consonants coming between two vowels .... `impor-tant`

8. Divide a hyphenated word only on the hyphen .... `self-esteem`

   Note: All words beginning with **self** are hyphenated, except **selfish**.

9. Do not divide a one-syllable word .... `passed`

10. Do not divide a word with fewer than 6 letters.

11. Do not divide these endings:
able	ible	sion
tion	cial	tial
cient	cious	eous

12. Do not divide a capitalized word .... `Chicago`

13. Do not divide a word unless you can carry at least 3 letters to the next line .... `bet-ter`

14. Do not separate: (a) mixed numbers .... `150 3/4`
    (b) sums of money .... `$125.50`

15. Do not separate one letter from the rest of a word. You cannot divide **about, around.**

16. Do not divide: (a) contractions .... `hasn't`
    (b) abbreviations .... `C.O.D.`

17. Avoid dividing the last word of a paragraph or page.

18. Avoid dividing the last word on the first line of a paragraph or page.

19. Avoid separating: (a) parts of a name .... `Sam Jones`
    (b) title from name .... `Dr. Jones`

20. Avoid dividing any word—if possible.

   When in doubt, find out: Consult the dictionary.

Rules for Word Division

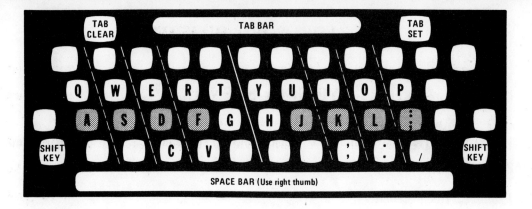

4. **New-Key Practice:** / (Slant)   *Use ;-Finger.*

Practice the reach from ; to / and back home to ;. Keep the **J** and **K**-fingers in home position. When you can reach the /-key without looking at your fingers, type each line twice:

c/o =
care of

c/l =
car lots

```
/ / / / ;/; ;/; ;/; c/o c/o; c/l c/l; s/s s/s s/s
;/; ;/; ;/; his/yours his/yours; we/they we/they;
```

s/s =
steamship

5. **Paragraph Practice:** Double Spaced
   A. Type each paragraph slowly, smoothly.
   B. Practice each word that has an error.
   C. Try for a PERFECT copy of each paragraph.

WORDS

Set your line-space regulator at "2."
```
        Skill grows at a quiet pace.  Hurry is waste.     10
Type at such a rate that you feel at perfect ease.        20
....1....2....3....4....5....6....7....8....9....10
```

```
        Type at a very steady pace, without pauses or     10
jerks.  This is how you will develop a good skill.        20
....1....2....3....4....5....6....7....8....9....10
```

6. **Test Your Skill:** Take Three 1-Minute Timings.
   Goal: 15 words a minute within 3 errors.
       Record your best speed within 3 errors.

Single-Spaced, Blocked Paragraph.
Set Line-Space Regulator at "1."

All the keys you know.
```
Dear Vicki:  Pat Garvy takes the speed test today.       10
Jud Quat is out of practice; he will try it later.        20
....1....2....3....4....5....6....7....8....9....10
```

Lesson 10: C V / (Slant)

TYPING A STENCIL

A **stencil** is a waxed-paper sheet from which duplicate copies are run off by a **mimeograph** machine.

To Produce a Good Stencil:
1. Type a model of the material on the same size paper you will use in running off the stencil.
2. Clean the type thoroughly with a stiff bristle brush moistened in typewriter cleaning fluid.
3. Set the ribbon-control lever on stencil.

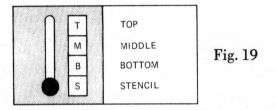

Fig. 19

4. Place the cushion sheet, glossy side up, between the stencil sheet and the backing sheet.
5. Insert the stencil carefully so that it does not wrinkle. Set the margin stops.
6. Type slowly, with a stroke sharp enough to make a clear-cut impression. Strike **w**, **m**, and all capitals with more force. Use less force on punctuation marks and the letters **a**, **e**, **o**, **c**. The electric machine makes a uniform impression automatically.
7. Proofread the stencil while it is still in the machine.

To Make a Good Correction:
1. Turn the cylinder up carefully to prevent wrinkling the stencil.
2. Rub the error lightly with the round end of the burnisher provided with the correction fluid, or the rounded end of a paper clip.
3. Apply a thin coating of correction fluid over the error and allow to dry.
4. Type the correction.

LESSON 11

NEW KEYS
B M X

MARGINS: 15-70 (Pica)
25-80 (Elite)
SPACING: Single

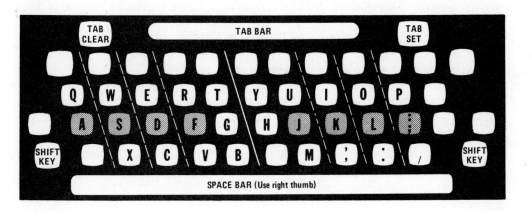

1. **Review:** Type each line twice. Double space after each 2-line group.

Line 3:
Zip D-finger
from C to E;
F-finger from
R to V without
pausing on
home key.

```
fr ju ft jy fg jh de ki sw lo aq ;p fv ;/ fv dc ;/
fist jerk cave hogs quit wade yule aqua kegs pelt;
vice vice vice slice slice slice curve curve curve
If you wish to keep a secret, keep it to yourself.
Every day is a good day if you put it to good use.
```

Try to type
each repeat
line a little
faster.

2. **New-Key Practice: B** *Use F-Finger.*

Practice the reach from **F** to **B** and back home to **F**. Keep the **A S D** fingers in home position. When you can reach **B** without looking at your fingers, type each line twice:

```
b b b b fbf fbf fbf fbf; but but but; bid bid bid;
fbf fbf fbf bag bag bag; boy boy boy; bow bow bow;
fbf fbf fbf bar bar bar; bus bus bus; cub cub cub;
lab lab; bug bug bug; fob fob fob; quibble quibble
hub web big buy pub rib jab rub tub ebb bake above
```

Strike
space bar
sharply.

3. **New-Key Practice: M** *Use J-Finger.*

Practice the reach from **J** to **M** and back home to **J**. Keep the **K L ;** fingers in home position. When you can reach **M** without looking at your fingers, type each line twice:

```
m m m m jmj jmj jmj jmj; mad mad mad; may may may;
jmj jmj jmj mug mug mug; mop mop mop; Mac Mac Mac;
jmj jmj jmj vim vim vim; hum hum hum; mal mal mal;
aim aim aim met met met; mow mow mow; rim rim rim;
gym mob mud gum jam sum him mar milk qualm flames;
```

Zip J-finger
from U to M;
from M to U
without paus-
ing on home
key.

LETTERS ARE REPRESENTATIVES

Every business letter is a representative of the company making a personal visit. So it should, first of all, make a good impression.

WHAT IS AN EFFECTIVE BUSINESS LETTER?

A business letter is effective to the extent that it is clear and concise and has the "you attitude."

BE CLEAR

A clear letter is quickly understood. "Know what you want to say; say it as simply as possible."[1]

BE CONCISE

Make every word count. Write plainly and directly. Omit unnecessary details.

TAKE THE "YOU ATTITUDE"

Show the reader that you want to do something about his needs and problems. As Albert C. Fries has said:

> Write from the reader's point of view.
> This rule emphasizes an attitude of
> service. It means that the writer must
> visualize the reader, his desires, his
> job, his probable reactions—and then
> plan the letter accordingly.[2]

---

1. J. C. Tressler, _et al._, _Business English in Action_, (Boston: D. C. Heath, 1949), page 49.

2. Albert C. Fries, _et al._, _Applied Secretarial Practice_, (New York: McGraw-Hill, 1957), page 199.

Note: "et al." means "and others."

4. **New-Key Practice: X** *Use S-Finger.*

Practice the reach from **S** to **X** and back home to **S**. Curl the **S**-finger as it reaches to **X**. Keep the **F**-finger in home position. When you can reach **X** without looking at your fingers, type each line twice:

```
x x x x  sxs sxs sxs sxs; six six six; tax tax tax;
sxs sxs sxs box box box; lax lax lax; wax wax wax;
pox pox pox vex vex vex; hex hex hex; axe axe axe;
fox fox fox Dix Dix Dix; Cox Cox Cox; Rex Rex Rex;
sex mix axe wax pox lax fox hex box flux Max Xmas;
```

Hold hands parallel to the slant of the keyboard.

5. **Paragraph Practice:** Double Spaced

Try for a PERFECT copy of each paragraph.

WORDS

```
        Aim to excel.  Do your daily task to the best        10
of your ability.  Good work leads to a happy life.           20
Remember:  Success comes if you strive quite hard.           30
....1....2....3....4....5....6....7....8....9....10
```

```
        To develop a skill takes time, of course.  So        10
devote as much time as possible to your daily work           20
here.  Have faith.  Expert skill will come to you.           30
....1....2....3....4....5....6....7....8....9....10
```

6. **Test Your Skill:** *Take Three 1-Minute Timings.*

Goal: 15 words a minute within 3 errors.

Record your best speed within 3 errors.

Single Spaced, Blocked Paragraph.
Set Line-Space Regulator at "1."

WORDS

All the keys you know.

```
Dear Paul:  Jack said he will meet you at the ball        10
game Friday.  Vic Quay will take you home by taxi.        20
....1....2....3....4....5....6....7....8....9....10
```

Lesson 11: B M X

MANUSCRIPT TYPING

1. PAPER:
    A. Use 8½ x 11 white bond.
    B. Type on 1 side only. Make at least 1 carbon copy.

2. SPACING:
    A. Double space all lines.
    B. Indent all paragraphs 5 spaces.

3. MARGIN STOPS:
    Pica: 15-75; Elite: 20-85

4. TOP MARGIN—PAGE 1
    2 inches: 12 lines
    A. Space down 13 single lines from top edge of the paper.
    B. Center the title in all capitals.
    C. Space down 3 single lines and start the first line in the copy.

5. TOP MARGIN—PAGE 2
    AND FOLLOWING PAGES
    1 inch: 6 lines
    A. Space down 7 single lines from top edge of the paper.
    B. Continue with the text.

6. BOTTOM MARGIN:
    1 inch on all pages
    A. Make a light pencil mark about 1½ inches from the bottom.
    B. Type 3 more lines after reaching this mark.

7. PARAGRAPH HEADINGS:
    A. Space down 3 single lines from last typewritten line.
    B. Start the paragraph heading at the margin—in all capitals.
    C. Double space and start paragraph.

8. QUOTATIONS
    3 lines or less:
    Type them in the same paragraph—within quotation marks.
    4 lines or more:
    Type them in a separate blocked paragraph—without quotation marks. Use short lines, single spacing.

9. PAGE NUMBERS:
    A. Do not number the first page.
    B. Type 2 on line 3 of second page—at the right margin.

10. FOOTNOTES:
    A. Type a 2-inch underscore 1 space below the last paragraph. Then double space and type the footnote—single spaced, indented. This way you leave 1 blank line above and below the underscore.
    B. Identify each footnote—type the same raised number shown in the text.
    C. Underscore book titles and magazine names. Use quotation marks for chapter titles and magazine articles.

These rules are illustrated by the model on the next page.

MARGINS: 15-70 (Pica)
25-80 (Elite)
SPACING: Single

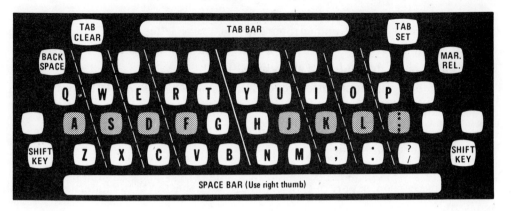

1. **Review:** Type each line twice. Double space after each 2-line group.

Line 4:
Zip F-finger from R to B; from B to T without pausing on home key.

```
abcd efgh ijkl mopq rstu vwxy abcd efgh ijkl mopq;
ark how eve box sue fly pad two hum jigs quit deck
A small boy with a watch has the time of his life.
verb verb verb curbs curbs curbs debts debts debts
much much much jumps jumps jumps rumor rumor rumor
```

Line 5:
Zip J-finger from M to U; from U to M without pausing on home key.

2. **New-Key Practice: Z** *Use A-Finger.*

Practice the reach from **A** to **Z** and back home to **A.** Curl the finger as it reaches down to **Z.** Keep the **F**-finger in home position. When you can reach **Z** without looking at your fingers, type each line twice:

```
z z z z aza aza aza aza; zig zig zig; zag zag zag;
aza aza aza zip zip zip; zoo zoo zoo; zed zed zed;
aza aza aza adz adz adz; fiz fiz fiz; amaze amaze;
blitz blitz blitz; tizzy tizzy tizzy; craze craze;
viz., zest jazz lazy Zeke quiz whizz zebra zephyr;
```

Fix each key location in your mind.

3. **New-Key Practice: N** *Use J-Finger.*

Practice the reach from **J** to **N** and back home to **J.** Keep the **K L** ; fingers in home position. When you can reach **N** without looking at your fingers, type each line twice:

All the alphabet keys.

```
n n n n jnj jnj jnj jnj; nil nil nil; sun sun sun;
jnj jnj jnj Ben Ben Ben; run run run; can can can;
jnj jnj jnj van van van; end end end; nix nix nix;
pen pen pen gun gun gun; now now now; ton ton ton;
won yen fun man gun hun din zinc junk links queen;
```

Zip J-finger from U to N; from N to U without pausing on home key.

CARBON COPIES

Business typists make at least one carbon copy of every letter. The carbon copy is usually a cheaper grade of paper—without a letterhead—known as a "second sheet."

1. Carbon paper has a dull side and shiny side.
2. The shiny side is put facing the second sheet on which the copy is to be made.

To Make One Carbon Copy:

1. Put a second sheet on the desk.
2. On top of it, put a carbon paper, shiny side down.
3. On top of the carbon paper, put an original letter sheet with the letterhead at the top, facing up.
4. Pick up the three sheets; straighten the top and sides; insert the set into the machine. If the edges are not even, depress the paper release lever and align the papers. Return the paper release lever back in place.
5. Check: Before typing, see that the shiny side of the carbon paper faces the second sheet.

To Make Several Carbon Copies at One Time:

1. Put a second sheet on the desk. On top of it, put a carbon paper, shiny side down. Repeat till you have the required number of second sheets.
2. Put an original letter sheet, face up, on top of the pack; straighten the top and sides.
3. Put an envelope with its flap over the top edge—to hold the papers in place.
4. Insert the pack. If it is too thick, depress the paper release lever and push the pack into the machine. Then remove the envelope and snap the paper release lever back in place.
5. Check: Before typing, see that the shiny side of each carbon paper faces the second sheet.

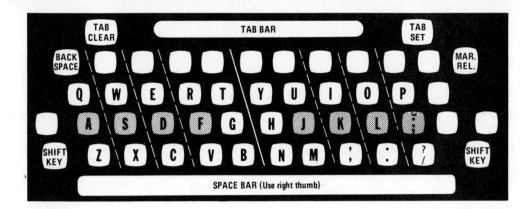

4. **New-Key Practice: ?** *Use ;-Finger*
The **?** is on the /-key. Practice the reach like this: (1) Depress left shift key; (**2**)
Reach for the /-key; (3) Zip fingers back home. When you can do these 3 steps
smoothly—without looking at your fingers—type each line twice:

*Space twice
after ? at
end of a
sentence.*

```
? ? ;?; ;?; ;?; Who? Who? Why? Why? Ben? Max? Vic?
Where is Zoel?  Where is Marvin?  Where is Robert?
```

5. **Paragraph Practice:** Double Spaced,
Try for a PERFECT copy of each paragraph.

WORDS

*All the
alphabet
keys.*

```
        You want to do well in some subject.  Why not     10
perfect your typing skill?  You can use your skill        20
in many small ways to help you in your daily work.        30
....1....2....3....4....5....6....7....8....9....10

        You can also use your typing skill as a means     10
of securing an office job.  It is a valuable skill        20
to have.  You can acquire it; exert a bit of zeal.        30
....1....2....3....4....5....6....7....8....9....10
```

6. **Test Your Skill:** *Take Three 1-Minute Timings.*
Goal: 15 words a minute within 3 errors.
Record your best speed within 3 errors.

Single Spaced, Blocked Paragraph.
Set Line-Space Regulator at "1."

WORDS

*All the
alphabet
keys.*

```
Mr. Querz:  Joel Knox will get the xerox copies by    10
Tuesday.  You will have five samples the same day.    20
....1....2....3....4....5....6....7....8....9....10
```

Lesson 12: Z N ?

SPREADING

Spreading is the process of inserting a word shorter by one letter than the one erased. Doing so leaves $1\frac{1}{2}$ spaces on each side of the new word, instead of the regular one space.

Error in second word.   `Please gives me the pen.`

1. Erase the whole word.   `Please     me the pen.`

2. Set the carriage at the point where you erased the second letter of the word.

3. Partly depress the backspace key; or press against the left knob, pushing the carriage back a half space. Type the letter **g**.   `Please g    me the pen.`

4. Set the carriage at the point where you erased the next letter of the word. Then partly depress the backspace key; or press against the left knob, pushing the carriage back a half space. Type the letter **i**.   `Please gi    me the pen.`

5. Repeat the routine for each remaining letter till you have typed the correct word.   `Please give me the pen.`

PIVOTING

Pivoting means typing one line so that it ends even with another line.

FOR EXAMPLE: You want line 2 to end even with line 1. `Richard Cassidy`
`                                                           Treasurer`

Follow These Steps:
1. Type line 1.
2. Set carriage one space after last letter in line 1.
3. Backspace once for each stroke in line 2.
4. Type line 2.

LESSON 13

NEW KEYS
(Hyphen)   Shift Lock

MARGINS: 15-70 (Pica)
25-80 (Elite)
SPACING: Single

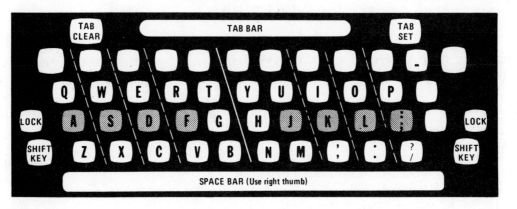

1. **Review:** Type each line twice. Double space after each 2-line group.

All the alphabet keys.

```
frf juj ftf jyj fgf jhj ded kik sws lol aqa ;p; ty
fvf jmj fbf jnj dcd k,k sxs l.l aza ;/; ;?; ;:; ;?
Skill is the result of quiet, day by day practice.
You must stay awake to make your dreams come true.
The quick brown fox jumped over the lazy old dogs.
```

Keep wrists low and relaxed but off the typewriter frame.

2. **New-Key Practice:** - (Hyphen)   *Use ;-Finger.*

Practice the reach from semicolon to hyphen and back home to semicolon. Straighten the ;-finger as it goes up for the hyphen. Keep the **J**-finger in home position. When you can reach the hyphen without looking at your fingers, type each line twice:

All the alphabet keys.

```
- - - ;-; ;-; ;-; ;-; one-half; one-half; one-half
;-; ;-; one-fifth; one-sixth; blue-gray; all-black
;-; ;-; zig-zag; part-time; half-price; by-product
;-; ;-; second-rate; son-in-law; up-to-date jacket
ice-clad; ready-made; quick-witted; vice-president
```

No space before or after a hyphen.

3. **New-Key Practice: Shift Lock**

The Shift Lock is above one or both of the shift keys. Use it to type a word or **group** of words in CAPITALS.

> For the left shift lock . . . use the *A*-finger.
> For the right shift lock . . . use the ;-finger.

(1) Press the shift lock;
     zip the finger home.
(2) Type the word or words.
(3) Release the lock—tap
     the opposite shift key.

CROWDING

Crowding is the process of inserting a word longer by one letter than the one typed.

Omission of a letter at the beginning or end of a word.

`Please giv me the pen.`

The correction is made by "crowding" the letter **e** into the half space after the letter **v**.

1. Move the carriage to the space after the letter **v**.

2. Partly depress the backspace key; or press against the left knob, pushing the carriage back a half space.

`Please give me the pen.`

Omission of a letter within a word.

`Please gve me the pen.`

1. Erase the whole word.

`Please      me the pen.`

2. Set the carriage in position to type the first erased letter.

3. Partly depress the backspace key; or press against the left knob, pushing the carriage back a half space. Type the first letter.

`Please g    me the pen.`

4. For each remaining letter, set the carriage in position; partly depress the backspace key; or press against the left knob, pushing the carriage back a half space. Type the letter.

`Please give me the pen.`

Type each line twice.

All the alphabet keys.

To type words in ALL CAPITALS, use the SHIFT LOCK.
Zoel Buxton is now typing SMOOTHLY and ACCURATELY.
Dear Jacqueline: Who types FASTER, Max or Victor?
See the expert BOUNCE his THUMB off the space bar.
DEXTERITY in any skill comes from PROPER PRACTICE.

Release the Shift Lock instantly after you have typed the word or words in ALL CAPITALS.

4. **Paragraph Practice:** Single Spaced, Blocked.
   Try for a PERFECT copy of each paragraph:

Hyphen used to divide a word at end of a line.

Dear Joe: Do you happen to know how far the equa-
tor is from Houston, Texas? What do you estimate?
....1....2....3....4....5....6....7....8....9....10

All the alphabet keys.

Dear Vera: I am glad to hear that your sister-in-
law passed the examination for high school teacher.
....1....2....3....4....5....6....7....8....9....10

Hyphen used to combine words into a "compound" word.

Dear Buzz: Did you know that Roxie Jimson--Shorty
to the class--won that school typewriting contest?
....1....2....3....4....5....6....7....8....9....10

2 hyphens used for a dash. No space before or after a dash.

5. **Test Your Skill:** *Take Three 1-Minute Timings.*
   Goal: 18 words a minute within 3 errors.
   Record your best speed within 3 errors.

WORDS

All the alphabet keys.

Dear Paul: Ask Jack Quin if he knows the chemical   10
symbols for carbon dioxide. Give me a buzz today.   20
....1....2....3....4....5....6....7....8....9....10

Lesson 13: - (Hyphen) and Shift Lock

ERASING

NOTE: A. On original copy, use a HARD eraser.

          B. On carbon copies, use a SOFT eraser.

          C. Clean the erasers by rubbing them on clean paper.

          D. Clean your hands.

1. Turn the paper till the error is on top of the roller.

2. Move the carriage to left or right so that eraser grit falls outside the machine.

3A. Erase the error on the last carbon copy FIRST—with the SOFT eraser. Then insert a strip of paper between the erasure and the shiny side of the carbon paper.

  B. Erase the error on the next carbon copy. Then insert another strip of paper between the erasure and the shiny side of the carbon copy.

  C. Continue this way till you reach the original copy.

4. Erase the error on the original copy with the HARD eraser. Use light, quick, up-and-down strokes, blowing the grit away from the machine.

5A. Remove the strips of paper.

  B. Return the carriage to the point where the erasure was made.

  C. Type the correction. If necessary, backspace and type it again until the letter is as dark as the others on the page.

Note: Stationary stores carry special devices for correcting errors.

LESSON 14
MARGIN RELEASE

MARGINS: 15-70 (Pica)
25-80 (Elite)
SPACING: Single

1. **Review:** Type each line twice. Double space after each 2-line group.

All the alphabet keys.

```
abcd efgh ijkl mnop qrst uvwx yzab cdef ghij klmno
feed back soap high flux over quit jazz words many
Kay Jim Ben Hub Cal Fox Liz Vic Dot Sam Row Queen;
The worst-tempered people are those who are wrong.
The machine can do anything--except get your food.
```

Stretch shift-key finger. Keep other fingers in typing position.

2. **Paragraph Practice:** Double Spacing.
   A. Type each paragraph twice—slowly, smoothly.
   B. Practice each word that has an error.
   C. Try for a PERFECT copy of each paragraph.

WORDS

```
     You are now able to type by touch.  This means       10
that you can type--without looking at your fingers.       20
....1....2....3....4....5....6....7....8....9....10
```

```
     The more you type by touch, the faster you can       10
type.  Soon, you will be a rapid, competent typist.       20
....1....2....3....4....5....6....7....8....9....10
```

```
     You will have a highly-valuable skill that you       10
can put to use in your personal and business tasks.       20
....1....2....3....4....5....6....7....8....9....10
```

ALIGNING

Aligning is the technique of inserting omitted letters after the paper has been removed.

1. Type the alphabet on a sheet of paper:

<u>abcdefghijklmnopqrstuvwxyz</u>
'''''''''''''''''''''''''''

Note how close the vertical white lines on YOUR aligning scale come to the center of the letters.

2. Type this name EXACTLY as shown: `Geo ge Wilkins n`

3. Remove the paper. Reinsert it. See that it is straight. Roll up the paper till the name is close to the aligning scale. Adjust the paper so that the white lines on the aligning scale point to the center of **i** and **l**. Use the paper release and the variable line spacer.

4. Move the carriage to the space for the **r** in Geo ge. Set ribbon control lever on stencil. Tap the **r**. The faint mark will show whether you need to make another adjustment. Return the lever to its normal position. Type the **r**. Then type the **o** in Wilkins n.

Too high: `Geo`^{r}`ge Wilkins`^{o}`n`

Too low: `Geo`$_r$`ge Wilkins`$_o$`n`

Just right: `George Wilkinson`

5. **Practice:** A. Type each line EXACTLY as shown:

```
J seph  J seph  J seph
Robe t  Robe t  Robe t
Wal er  Wal er  Wal er
```

B. Remove the paper. Reinsert and align it.
C. Type the missing **o r t**.

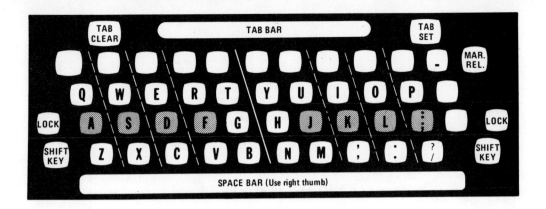

3. **Margin Release:** Sometimes you may find it necessary to type a few letters beyond your right margin stop. For example: In paragraph 3-A below, the lines extend beyond 70 (Pica); 80 (Elite). So when you hear the margin bell—

(1) Type on until the keys lock.
(2) Press Margin Release key at top of keyboard, right or left.
(3) Finish typing the line.

Practice: Type 2 copies of paragraph 3-A.

3-A.

Double Spacing.

      The many different makes and models of typewriters have different means of setting margin stops. Study your machine to determine how to adjust the stops quickly like an expert.

4. **Test Your Skill:** *Take Three 1-Minute Timings.*
   Goal: 15 words a minute within 3 errors.
      Record your best speed within 3 errors.

                                                                                     WORDS

All the alphabet keys.

      Paul visited Rex and Zolie when they got back   10

from Japan and Iraq and heard about their voyages.   20
....1....2....3....4....5....6....7....8....9....10

TYPING ON LINES

In your business or personal work, you may often have to type on lines. To do so:

1. Push in or pull out the variable line spacer—the button in the left knob, and roll the cylinder to bring the line into correct position for typing.

2. Test the position of the line: Set the ribbon control lever for stencil and tap one underscore. The light line it makes tells you whether to roll the paper up or down.

3. Reset the ribbon control lever to its original position. Then type.

EXAMPLES: This is too high.
‾‾‾‾‾‾‾‾‾‾‾‾‾‾‾‾‾
This is too low.

This is just right.

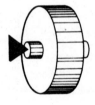

Fig. 17c. Variable Line Spacer.

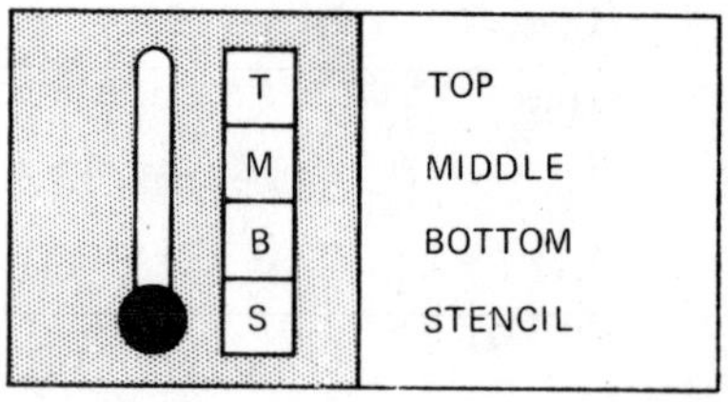

Fig. 18. Ribbon Control Lever.

T	TOP	
M	MIDDLE	
B	BOTTOM	
S	STENCIL	

LESSON 15
NEW KEYS
1 3 7

MARGINS: 15-70 (Pica)
25-80 (Elite)
SPACING: Single

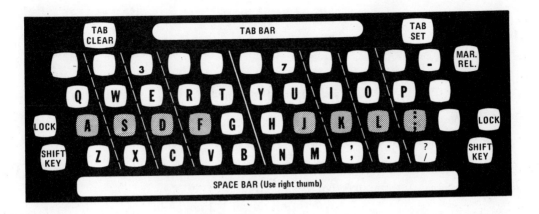

1. **Review:** Type each line twice. Double space after each 2-line group.

abcd efgh ijkl mnop qrst uvwx yzab cdef ghij klmno
hope quiz foxy back melt dent rust high vows jokes
Marriage must be wonderful; so many people try it.
Most children take advice--then do as they please.
The quiz Jay picked for six big men will vex them.

All the alphabet keys.

2. **New-Key Practice: 1**
   If you have a **1** key on top row, use **A**-finger.
   If you have no **1** key, type the small **L** for **1**.

Type each line twice:

ala ala ala ala Add 1 and 1 and 11 and 11 and 111.
11 acts 11 apes 11 axes 11 lads 11 loads 11 lamps;
Cal will be 1 year and 11 months old next June 11.
We need 11 pairs of size 11 socks for the 11 boys.
Bus No. 11 on Route 11 is due to arrive in 1 hour.

Relax your shoulders. Let your arms hang loosely at your sides.

3. **New-Key Practice: 3** *Use D-Finger.*
   Practice the reach from **D** to **3** and back home to **D**. Keep the **F**-finger at home. When you can reach **3** without looking at your fingers, type each line twice:

3 3 3 d3d d3d d3d 3 and 31 and 113 and 131 and 313
3 days 3 dogs 3 dads; 33 dolls 33 dishes 33 dukes;
Donald and his 3 pals caught 13 fish on August 31.
For the next quiz, read pages 3, 13, 31, 131, 133.
Ben Cox will be 13 years 3 months old December 31.

Think the finger and the number it controls.

15. Paragraph
1. Type a capital **P**;
2. Backspace;
3. Type a small **l**.

Revision of ₽3

16. Section
1. Type a capital **S**;
2. Backspace;
3. Turn roller down slightly and type capital **S** again.

Revision of §3

17. Military zero
1. Type a regular **O**;
2. Backspace;
3. Type a slant.

Start at Ø2ØØ.

18. Brackets

Left Bracket
1. Turn roller down 1 line and type an underscore;
2. Turn roller up 1 line and backspace twice;
3. Type a slant;
4. Backspace once and type an underscore.

Right Bracket
1. Turn roller down 1 line and type an underscore;
2. Turn roller up 1 line and backspace once;
3. Type a slant;
4. Backspace twice and type an underscore.

She ╱Pat Hix╱

19. Bar graph line
Type small **m** in a solid row.

mmmmmmmmmmmmmm

20. Fractions not on keyboard
1. Type number and slant.
2. Space after the whole number if fraction is made.
3. Do not space after the whole number if fraction is on keyboard.
4. If one fraction in a sentence is made, all of them must be made.

3/4, 5/6, 7/9

3 4/5, 10 3/7

2¼, 10½, 125½

2/3, 1/4, 1/2

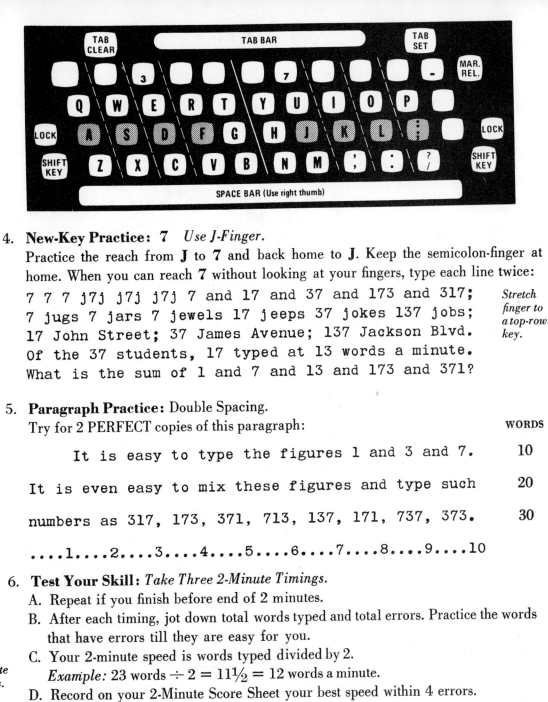

4. **New-Key Practice: 7** *Use J-Finger.*

Practice the reach from **J** to **7** and back home to **J**. Keep the semicolon-finger at home. When you can reach **7** without looking at your fingers, type each line twice:

```
7 7 7 j7j j7j j7j 7 and 17 and 37 and 173 and 317;
7 jugs 7 jars 7 jewels 17 jeeps 37 jokes 137 jobs;
17 John Street; 37 James Avenue; 137 Jackson Blvd.
Of the 37 students, 17 typed at 13 words a minute.
What is the sum of 1 and 7 and 13 and 173 and 371?
```

Stretch finger to a top-row key.

5. **Paragraph Practice:** Double Spacing.

Try for 2 PERFECT copies of this paragraph:

WORDS

```
     It is easy to type the figures 1 and 3 and 7.        10

It is even easy to mix these figures and type such        20

numbers as 317, 173, 371, 713, 137, 171, 737, 373.        30
....1....2....3....4....5....6....7....8....9....10
```

6. **Test Your Skill:** *Take Three 2-Minute Timings.*

Follow these steps in all your 2-minute timings.

A. Repeat if you finish before end of 2 minutes.

B. After each timing, jot down total words typed and total errors. Practice the words that have errors till they are easy for you.

C. Your 2-minute speed is words typed divided by 2.
   Example: 23 words ÷ 2 = 11½ = 12 words a minute.

D. Record on your 2-Minute Score Sheet your best speed within 4 errors.
   Goal: 18 words a minute within 4 errors.

WORDS

```
     Fix your mind on what you are typing.  Start          10

at a slow pace and gradually work up to your best          20

speed.  Do not type so fast that you lose control.         30

Typing speed grows like a baby--slowly, gradually.         40
....1....2....3....4....5....6....7....8....9....10
```

Lesson 15: 1 3 7

SPECIAL SYMBOLS

NAME	HOW MADE	EXAMPLE
1. Times or By sign	Type a small **x**	What is 7 x 9? a 10 x 15 rug
2. Equal sign	1. Type a hyphen; 2. Backspace; 3. Turn roller up slightly by hand and type hyphen again. (Some machines have the = key.)	10 x 10 = 100
3. Plus sign	1. Type a hyphen; 2. Backspace; 3. Type a slant (Some machines have the + key)	90 $\neq$ 10 = 100
4. Minus sign	Type a hyphen.	100 - 10 = 90
5. Division sign	1. Type a hyphen; 2. Backspace; 3. Type a colon.	100 ÷ 10 = 10
6. Degree sign	Turn roller down slightly by hand and type a small **o**.	Temperature 9°
7. Raised number	Turn roller down slightly by hand and type the number.	$x^2 - y^3 - xy^3$
8. Lowered number	Turn roller slightly up by hand and type the number.	H_2O is water.
9. Feet and inches (after numbers)	Apostrophe for feet. Quotation mark for inches.	Length is 10' Length is 10"
10. Minutes, seconds (after numbers)	Apostrophe for minutes; Quotation mark for seconds.	Maxie ran the mile in 5' 3".
11. Caret	1. Type an underscore and a slant; 2. Center the inserted word above the slant.	the Hy made/team.
12. Pounds (British money)	1. Type a small **f**; 2. Backspace; 3. Type a capital **L**.	Price is £10
13. Roman numerals	Type capital letters.	I V X L C D M
14. Star	1. Type a small **v**; 2. Backspace; 3. Type a capital **A**.	✭ ✭ ✭ ✭ ✭

LESSON 16
NEW KEYS
2 6

MARGINS: 15-70 (Pica)
25-80 (Elite)
SPACING: Single

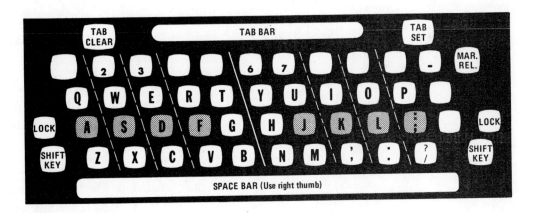

1. **Review:** Type each line twice. Double space after each 2-line group.

abcd efgh ijkl mnop qrst uvwx yzab cdef ghij klmno
jazz back your sure high view lone deft quip exams
Relatives you inherit, but friends you can select.
all all all d3d d3d d3d j7j j7j j7j 1 and 3 and 73
What is the sum of 1 and 3 and 17 and 371 and 713?

Return carriage quickly-- without looking up.

2. **New-Key Practice: 2** *Use S-Finger.*
Practice the reach from **S** to **2** and back home to **S**. Try to keep the **F**-finger in home position. When you can reach **2** without looking at your fingers, type each line twice:

2 2 2 s2s s2s s2s 2 steps 2 seals 2 shops 2 stones
2 ships 2 sails 2 sizes 2 skirts 2 shapes 2 spaces
June 27, 1232; September 12, 1272; August 23, 1322
Cora Dix will be 12 years 2 months old January 27.
Add these figures: 2, 12, 21, 23, 27, 32, and 72.

Space twice after a colon.

3. **New-Key Practice: 6** *Use J-Finger.*
Practice the reach from **J** to **6** and back home to **J**. Stretch the **J**-finger up and to the left. Keep the semicolon-finger home. When you can reach **6** without looking at your fingers, type each line twice:

6 6 6 j6j j6j j6j 6 jumps 6 jails 6 jeeps 6 jests;
6 jades 6 jaunts 6 jacks 6 juries 6 jewels 6 jobs;
August 6, 1627; October 3, 1632; November 12, 1766
What is the sum of 21 and 63 and 27 and 16 and 26?
Maxie paid 62 cents for 16 stamps he used June 26.

COMMON ERRORS IN MACHINE OPERATION

	ERROR	CAUSE	REMEDY
1.	Raised Capitals	Releasing shift key too soon.	Hold shift key down till you have typed the capital letter.
2.	Blurred Letters	Not releasing the keys instantly.	On a Manual Machine, use short, sharp pecks. On an Electric Machine, lightly tap-and-release the keys.
3.	Uneven Left Margin	Returning the carriage weakly, or with too much force.	On a Manual Machine, flip the return lever. On an Electric Machine, zip "pinky" to RETURN key and wait till the carriage stops.
4.	Omission or Insertion of Words	Looking up from the copy, causing you to lose the place.	Keep your eyes on the copy all the time. Use will power.
5.	Uneven Indenting	Not holding the tab key or tab bar down until carriage has stopped.	Hold the tab key or bar down firmly until carriage has stopped.
6.	Overlapping Letters and Spaces	Typing jerkily, causing strokes to miss their normal spacing.	Type evenly, smoothly, at a steady pace. Do not rush.
7.	Omission of Space or Leaving an Extra Space	Probably holding your thumb on space bar, or leaning your palm on machine.	Hold thumb $\frac{1}{2}$ inch above space bar and wrists $\frac{1}{2}$ inch above machine. Bounce thumb off space bar. Keep palms off machine.
8.	Reversing Letters	Reading too far ahead of your typing.	Fix eyes on the copy. If necessary, spell the words to yourself.
9.	Double Impressions	Pushing or pounding the keys.	On a Manual Machine, snap-and-release keys instantly. On an Electric Machine, tap keys lightly.
10.	Dark and Light Letters	Not striking all the keys with equal force.	On a Manual Machine, snap all the keys with equal force. The Electric Machine makes a uniform impression automatically.

4. **Paragraph Practice:** Double Spacing.

Try for a PERFECT copy of each paragraph:

WORDS

One space between a whole number and a "made" fraction.

	WORDS
You can make any fraction that is not on your	10
keyboard by typing the /. For example: 2/3, 1/6,	20
6/7, 1/3, 3/16, 2 1/7, 6 2/3, 3 6/7, 2 1/6, 7 1/12	30
....1....2....3....4....5....6....7....8....9....10	

	WORDS
Business typists use the / to shorten certain	10
terms in invoices. For example, they type B/L for	20
Bill of Lading; A/C for Account; N/C for No Charge.	30
....1....2....3....4....5....6....7....8....9....10	

WORDS

All the alphabet keys plus all the numbers you know.

	WORDS
Maxie, Buzz, and Vicki read pages 26, 31, and	10
62; they worked out problems 2, 6, 37, and 62 just	20
in time to hand them to Prof. Quimby before class.	30
Maxie, Buzz, and Vicki are pals and work together.	40
....1....2....3....4....5....6....7....8....9....10	

5. **Test Your Skill:** *Take Three 2-Minute Timings.*

Goal: 18 words a minute within 4 errors.

Record your best speed within 4 errors.

WORDS

Use double spacing.

	WORDS
Expert typing is not only a matter of moving	10
your fingers fast but also one of knowing all the	20
gadgets on the machine that help boost your speed.	30
So aim to develop their use with the utmost skill.	40
....1....2....3....4....5....6....7....8....9....10	

THE CITY

The city is, no doubt, the biggest thing that	10
man has built. But not all people think of cities	20
in the same way. To some, the city means glamour,	30
excitement, opportunity, wealth. To others, it is	40
a place of noise, slums, crime, poverty, and over-	50
crowding. So it seems that to one group, the city	60
is a lure--drawing people to it; to another, it is	70
a place to be avoided--except for doing business.	80

Of course, the great mass of the people knows   90
that neither of these ways of thinking of the city   100
is entirely right or entirely wrong. For the city   110
is highly complex, perhaps quite as complicated as   120
anything on earth. The solution to the variety of   130
problems that daily beset the city eludes our best   140
minds. Yet every candidate for mayor assumes that   150
he has the solution; all he asks is to be elected.   160
...1....2....3....4....5....6....7....8....9....10

CHOOSING A CAREER

The choice of a career is not an easy matter.   10
Tests cannot give a positive answer concerning the   20
career you should choose. You are too complex for   30
accurate and complete analysis. A test that shows   40
you are capable of doing a certain type of work is   50
no proof that you will be happy doing it. For the   60
choice of a career depends on a variety of factors.   70

The most important factors are your likes and   80
dislikes. So it seems you have to choose your own   90
career. No one can make the choice for you. Your   100
need for ready money might force you to accept the   110
first job offered. Such necessity should not kill   120
your drive to seek the kind of job you are set on.   130
You can still climb your way, little by little, to   140
that job. Make sure your choice is an intelligent   150
one. Then equip yourself for that sort of career.   160
...1....2....3....4....5....6....7....8....9....10

LESSON 17
NEW KEYS
5 9

MARGINS: 15-70 (Pica)
25-80 (Elite)
SPACING: Single

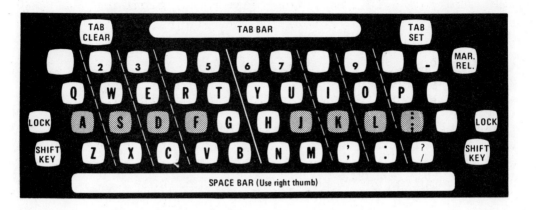

1. **Review:** Type each line twice. Double space after each 2-line group.

```
abcd efgh ijkl mnop qrst uvw xyz abcd efgh ijkl mn
back high jury dogs list from quip wavy zone axes;
Fortune smiles on the few--and laughs at the many.
all all s2s s2s j6j j6j d3d d3d j7j j7j 1 2 3 6 27
What is the sum of 12 and 37 and 16 and 73 and 62?
```

Use the correct finger for each number.

2. **New-Key Practice:** 5 *Use F-Finger.*
Practice the reach from **F** to **5** and back home to **F**. Keep the **A**-finger at home. When you can reach 5 without looking at your fingers, type each line twice:

```
5 5 5 f5f f5f f5f 5 flags 5 flaps 5 fires 55 files
5 figs 5 fish 5 flew 5 fads 5 fix 5 fled 55 frames
Of the 25 students, 16 typed at 37 words a minute.
On June 1, there were 35 big ships in Fleet No. 5.
The correct answer to problem 52 is 5 3/5 exactly.
```

No. is the abbreviation for number. Space once after an abbreviation.

3. **New-Key Practice:** 9 *Use L-Finger.*
Practice the reach from **L** to **9** and back home to **L**. Try to keep the **J**-finger at home. When you can reach **9** without looking at your fingers, type each line twice:

```
9 9 9 l9l l9l l9l 9 lamps 9 loads 9 lambs 9 ladies
9 lids 9 legs 9 laws 9 lots 9 laps 9 lads 9 lights
Only 16 of the 59 typists made final grades of 95.
What is the sum of 19 and 25 and 36 and 73 and 95?
At 9:15 a.m., May 9, I flew to Paris on Flight 59.
```

No space after period between small initials.

A MAGIC TRICK

	WORDS

Do you enjoy magic tricks? Here is one trick 10
you will enjoy trying out on some of your friends: 20

Ask the friend to jot down his age on a piece 30
of paper; then say that you will guess his correct 40
age if he will do as follows: Multiply the number 50
by two and add four to the answer. Then, multiply 60
by three and divide by six. Ask to see the number 70
your friend now has. Subtract two from the number 80
and you will then tell the person his correct age. 90

Example: The person's age is 19. Ask him or 100
her to multiply it by 2; that makes it 38; 38 plus 110
4 is 42; 42 times 3 is 126; 126 divided by 6 is 21; 120
21 minus 2 is age 19. Try to memorize these steps 130
exactly. It would spoil the fun to read them from 140
a memo. The trick works with any number selected. 150
....1....2....3....4...5....6....7....8....9....10

LEARN TO READ FASTER

	WORDS

Anyone who can read can learn to read faster. 10
You do not need a keen mind for reading speed. An 20
education helps but if you have a reasonably large 30
vocabulary, you really don't need formal education. 40

The slow readers have a tendency to read word 50
by word; they devote full attention to every word. 60
Instead, they should look only for the meaning of 70
groups of words. The words the author uses to put 80
his ideas across are not important. In fact, many 90
of them can be cut out without loss of the meaning. 100

A piece of writing, if of any merit, consists 110
of ideas and details that support those ideas. So 120
try to get the meaning by reading for ideas. Also 130
note the logical sequence with which the ideas are 140
presented--to help you grasp those ideas quickly. 150
....1....2....3....4....5....6....7....8....9....10

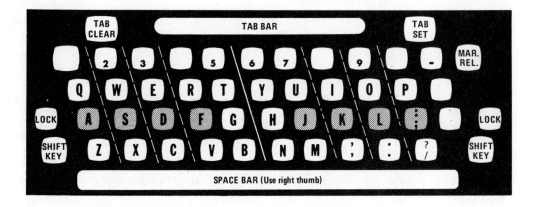

4. **Paragraph Practice:** Double Spacing.
   Try for 2 PERFECT copies of this note:

                                                               WORDS

		WORDS
All the alphabet keys plus all the numbers you know.	Dear Zoel:	2
	Up to now, I sold 9 tickets for the August 25	12
	game. Val Fox and Joe Quin sold 17; Pat, 16; Ben,	22
	13; and Cy, 12. This makes a total of 67 tickets.	32
	Tell coach Yardley that we are ahead of our quota.	42

....1....2....3....4....5....6....7....8....9....10

5. **Test Your Skill:** *Take Three 2-Minute Timings.*
   Goal: 18 words a minute within 4 errors.
          Record your best speed within 4 errors.

                                                             WORDS

   When you take a job, you become a member of a   10

working team. These people are quite important to   20

you.. Their help is vital to your own success. So   30

cooperate with them; work with zeal and good humor.   40

....1....2....3....4....5....6....7....8....9....10

BE A BETTER TYPIST

	WORDS
Be a better typist--follow these suggestions:	10
First, correct technique at the machine--sit erect	20
as tall as you can, feet flat on floor, eyes fixed	30
on the copy. Snap all keys on the manual machine;	40
tap them very lightly on the electric. Return the	50
carriage quickly, with eyes held on the copy. Be-	60
gin each line without pausing--without looking up.	70
Second, keep your mind only on the matter you	80
are typing. Pass quickly from word to word but do	90
not read ahead. Just type at an even, steady pace	100
without jerks. This way you develop accuracy plus	110
speed--the two basic elements of competent typing.	120
Third, learn to use every labor-saving device	130
on your machine just as the expert does--by touch.	140

....1....2....3....4....5....6....7....8....9....10

THE STORY OF KING MIDAS

	WORDS
In olden times, long, long ago, there lived a	10
King named Midas. He lived in a beautiful palace.	20
He had a pretty wife and a pretty daughter whom he	30
dearly loved, and lots of money to buy everything.	40
Yet this king was not happy. He was a miser.	50
He loved money for its own sake. In a secret room	60
in his palace he kept all his gold. He spent each	70
day counting over and over again his golden hoard.	80
One day he asked the Greek god named Dionysus	90
to grant him the wish of his life--that everything	100
he touched might turn to gold; and it was granted.	110
But King Midas, when he saw even his food changed	120
to gold, had to beg the god to take his gift back.	130
The story of King Midas is a myth, a fanciful	140
tale that has come down to us from many ages past.	150

...1....2....3....4....5....6....7....8....9....10

LESSON 18
NEW KEYS
4 8 0

MARGINS: 15-70 (Pica)
25-80 (Elite)
SPACING: Single

1. **Review:** Type each line twice. Double space after each 2-line group.

```
very buzz stew code flax ruse high main joke quips
Tact is the knack of making others do it your way.
f5f j6j s2s j7j l9l d3d 12 765 319 253 691 932 257
On June 23, 1957, we flew to Mexico on Flight 269.
President James K. Polk was born November 2, 1795.
```

Try to start each line without a pause.

2. **New-Key Practice: 4** *Use F-Finger.*
   Practice the reach from **F** to **4** and back home to **F**. Keep the **A**-finger at home. When you can reach **4** without looking at your fingers, type each line twice:

```
4 4 4 f4f f4f f4f 4 flaps 4 flags 4 fires 4 firms;
4 figs 4 furs 4 fish 4 files 4 facts 4 farms 144.4
About 44 boys took the 14-mile hike June 14, 1944.
Add these figures:  4 and 14 and 49 and 64 and 74.
The 14 boys caught the 4:15 p.m. train on Track 4.
```

3. **New-Key Practice: 8** *Use K-Finger.*
   Practice the reach from **K** to **8** and back home to **K**. Keep semicolon-finger in home position. When you can reach **8** without looking at your fingers, type each line twice:

```
8 8 8 k8k k8k k8k 8 knots 8 knobs 8 kites 8 kinds;
8 keys 8 kings 8 kits 8 kids 8 kegs 8 killed 48.14
What is the sum of 8 and 48 and 84 and 88 and 418?
The 84 men worked a total of 484 hours on July 18.
Vic will call tomorrow at 8:15 A. M. or 4:15 P. M.
```

Space once after period following capital initials.

WORKING FOR A LIVING

You want a place in which to live, the proper	10
food, clothing, and all the other things that make	20
for comfort and convenience and life worth living.	30
But all the things you desire you cannot have just	40
for the asking. You simply have to work for them.	50
Yet, at one time each family had to depend on	60
its own effort for all the things it needed. Each	70
family made its own clothing, raised its own food,	80
and put aside a sufficient surplus for the winter.	90
Now, each person makes a living by performing	100
special work for which he or she is paid in money.	110
With this money we all can get the things we need.	120

....1....2....3....4....5....6....7....8....9....10

CARE OF THE TYPEWRITER

Your typewriter will give you good service if	10
you take good care of it. Good care avoids expen-	20
sive repairs and gives your machine a longer life.	30
Here are a few things to do every day to keep	40
your machine working at top efficiency: Clean the	50
ink and dirt from type bars with a bristle brush.	60
Clean other parts with the long-handled typewriter	70
brush. Wipe upper and lower parts of the carriage	80
rail with a cloth. Remove dust from under machine.	90
Cover the machine when you have finished your work.	100
Once a week clean the type with type cleaner.	110
Clean cylinder and feed rolls with denatured alco-	120
hol. Spread a drop or two of oil on carriage rail.	130

....1....2....3....4....5....6....7....8....9....10

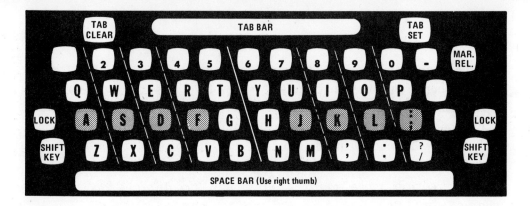

4. **New-Key Practice: 0** *Use Semicolon-Finger*

Practice the reach from semicolon to **0** and back home to semicolon. Keep the **J**-finger at home. Keep elbow close to body. When you can reach **0** without looking at your fingers, type each line twice.

```
0 0 0 ;0; ;0; ;0; 10 pins 10 pals 10 pads 10 packs
10 pets 10 pews 10 pegs 10 plums 10 plays 10 plans
The teams will practice at 10:30 a.m. or 2:30 p.m.
There were 150 to 170 men at the March 10 meeting.
Buzzy is 10 years 10 months and 10 days old today.
```

5. **Paragraph Practice:** Double Spacing.

Try for 2 PERFECT copies of this note:

WORDS

The whole alphabet and all the numbers.

	WORDS
Dear Walt:	2
I have arranged to have the Annual Banquet of	12
The Commercial Club meet at the Duke Hotel on June	22
9 at 8:00 p.m. in Room 1364. I expect at least 25	32
of our members to attend. Please manage to return	42
all unsold tickets to Mr. Zims by Tuesday, June 7.	52

```
....1....2....3....4....5....6....7....8....9....10
```

6. **Test Your Skill:** *Take Three 2-Minute Timings.*

Goal: 18 words a minute within 4 errors.

        Record your best speed within 4 errors.

WORDS

Use double spacing.

	WORDS
Frank E. McGurrin was the first touch typist.	10
In 1886 he won the first typing contest ever held.	20
He typed for 45 minutes at the speed of 98 words a	30
minute. He was also an expert shorthand reporter.	40

```
....1....2....3....4....5....6....7....8....9....10
```

7. Type evenly, smoothly; keep the carriage moving.
8. Type short, common words like *the, had,* without spelling them (t h e) (h a d). Flash them as a unit (the) (had).
9. Fix your mind only on the work you are doing.
10. To help you avoid frequent errors on certain letters, figures, symbols, practice the appropriate Keyboard Mastery Drills on pages 108-9.

HONESTY

	WORDS
You may have heard about Diogenes, a wise man	10
of ancient Greece. On one occasion he walked down	20
the streets of his home town at mid-day carrying a	30
lighted lantern. When asked for an explanation of	40
such strange conduct, he said that he was out look-	50
ing for an honest man.	55
People began to laugh and shake their heads--	65
they thought there was surely something wrong with	75
him. But Diogenes was, without doubt, quite sane.	85
He was trying to dramatize the fact that honesty in	95
his day was a rare virtue. And even now in our own	105
day and age, it appears that honesty is not common.	115

....1....2....3....4....5....6....7....8....9....10

THE FIRST JOB

TEST 2

	WORDS
When a student gets that first job upon grad-	10
uation, he or she soon finds out that the boss is	20
a lot more exacting in many matters than was that	30
patient and obliging teacher all liked at school.	40
The boss wants given work completed on time.	50
He doesn't always grant an extension of time when	60
work is due. He doesn't permit frequent lateness	70
or absence. He expects prompt arrival on the job.	80
The employer pays for the time and services	90
of an employee, never tolerates job laziness and	100
always expects full value for the salary he pays.	110
You will agree that this is indeed a fair demand.	120

....1....2....3....4....5....6....7....8....9....10

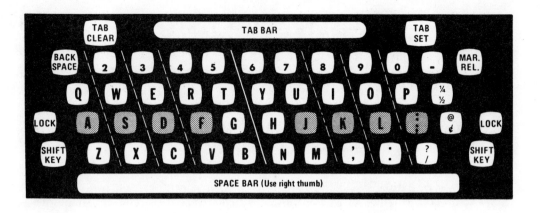

1. **Review:** Type each line twice. Double space after each 2-line group.

```
abcd efgh ijkl mnop qrst uvwx yzab cdef ghij klmno
Peg Biff Walt Chuck Viola Roxie Queen James Dizzy;
Use all your brains and even those you can borrow.
f4 j7 f5 j6 d3 k8 s2 l9 ;0 ;- ;/ 2/3, 5/6, l0 7/8;
The March 7 quiz covered pages 27, 31, 54, 68, 90.
```

All the alphabet and number keys.

2. **Horizontal Centering:** Horizontal centering means typing a word or line so that half of it is on each side of the center of the paper.

A. Standard typing paper is 8½ inches wide.

B. Pica type (large) measures 10 spaces to an inch.
   So: 8½ inches x 10 = 85 Pica spaces across the paper.

C. Elite type (small) measures 12 spaces to an inch.
   So: 8½ inches x 12 = 102 Elite spaces across the paper.

D. The center of 8½-inch paper is 42 (Pica); 50 (Elite).

To Center Horizontally:

A. Clear the machine. Set a tab stop at the center of the paper.

B. Insert the paper with its left edge at "0" on the paper guide scale.

C. Tabulate to the center of the paper— hold down the tab bar or tab key till the carriage stops.

D. Backspace once for every 2 letters, numbers, punctuation marks, or spaces in the line. Say the strokes in pairs depressing the backspacer once as you say each pair. Do not backspace for an odd letter at the end.

E. Begin typing when you finish backspacing.

5-MINUTE TIMED TESTS
(Pages 113 to 117)

Before You Take a Test:
1. Clear the machine.
2. Set margin stops: 15-70 (Pica); 25-80 (Elite).
3. Set line-space regulator for double spacing.

Test Procedure: (Take one test a day.)
1. Start with Test 1. Take three 5-minute timings. Repeat if you finish before end of 5 minutes.
2. After each timing, jot down total words typed and total errors.
3. Practice the words that have errors till they are easy for you.
4. Select your best speed within 5 errors.

Score Your Tests:
1. Make out a new 5-Minute Score Sheet like the one on page 160. Use the following headings:

Best Speed
within 5
errors ____

Goal:

```
5-MINUTE SCORE SHEET
     T E S T S

  1 2 3 4 5 6 7 8 9 10
```

2. Fill in your goal: 5 words a minute higher than your present speed. Then count down the column, writing the figures till you reach your LOWEST speed.
3. Record your best speed in Test 1. With Test 2, start joining the scores and watch your progress.
4. If you reach your goal before Test 10, make out a fresh score sheet. Set your new goal at 5 words a minute higher than before. Start over again with Test 1.

Skill-Booster Tips:
1. *Manual Machine:* Curve fingers deeply; rest them lightly on home keys. Snap the keys sharply, quickly.
2. *Electric Machine:* Curve fingers slightly; hold them as close as possible to home keys—without touching them. Tap the keys very lightly.
3. Move the fingers only. Try not to move wrists, elbows, arms.
4. Keep your eyes on the copy at all times.
5. Return the carriage without looking up. Begin a new line quickly.
6. Speed up the shift-key stroke. Do it in a continuous 1-2-3 motion: ONE, depress shift key. TWO, hold it down while you strike the correct key. THREE, release shift key, zip finger back home.

EXAMPLES:

A. *To center the word* TYPING:
1. Tabulate to the center of the paper.
2. Backspace once for every 2 letters:

TY PI NG

3. Type the word.

B. *To center the word* SHORTHAND:
1. Tabulate to the center of the paper.
2. Backspace once for every 2 letters:

Fig. 17 Using the Backspace Key

SH OR TH AN (Do not backspace for D)

3. Type the word.

C. *To center the words* BUSINESS TRAINING:
1. Tabulate to the center of the paper.
2. Backspace once for every 2 letters and spaces:

BU SI NE SS space T RA IN IN
(Do not backspace for G)

3. Type the words.

CHECK: The words in Examples A B C, when centered, should appear like this:

TYPING
SHORTHAND
BUSINESS TRAINING

3. **Centering Practice:** A. Center each line in each group.
B. Double space after each group.

Accuracy   Efficiency
Touch Typing   The Merit System
Horizontal Centering   Success in Business

Stenography   The Empire State Building
Transcription   34th Street and Fifth Avenue
Office Manager   New York, New York

SPEED BOOSTERS

One good way to boost your speed is to type easy sentences over and over. They help you type smoothly—to keep going without pausing.

Practice each sentence till you can type it PERFECTLY in the time you select. Your words-per-minute speed is given under that time.

Time in Seconds:	15	30	45	60
Words-per-Minute:	40	20	13	10

WORDS: ....1....2....3....4....5....6....7....8....9....10

1. A man with a bald head is one who came out on top.
2. You can get there faster with push than with pull.
3. What gives money its value is the work you put in.
4. Bury your past; but make sure it cannot be dug up.
5. Men at the top first went to the bottom of things.
6. Age brings wisdom but gives little time to use it.
7. The best time to save money is when you have some.
8. Anyone can take a day off; no one can put it back.
9. The folks who talk the most have the least to say.
10. A miser is a man who gets his money the hoard way.
11. Never put things off; better try to put them over.
12. Smart gals keep on their toes and away from heels.
13. The quick way to get ahead is to be born with one.
14. Talk may be cheap, but not when you hire a lawyer.
15. Love is what makes a park bench as soft as a sofa.
16. We drink to the health of others and ruin our own.
17. Ideas must work or they are not better than dreams.
18. A pretty face often has a lot of brains behind it.
19. Any nook is a home only if the family stays in it.
20. Time heals all wounds but cannot remove the scars.

....1....2....3....4....5....6....7....8....9....10

4. **Paragraph Practice:** Double Spacing.
   A. Type each paragraph twice—slowly, smoothly.
   B. Practice each word that has an error.
   C. Try for a PERFECT copy of each paragraph.

All the number keys.

Christopher Sholes, born on February 14, 1819,	10
made the first practical typewriter. He got a pat-	20
ent for his machine in 1868. Touch typing, though,	30
was first introduced in 1878 by Frank E. McGurrin.	40

....1....2....3....4....5....6....7....8....9....10

Oliver Wendell Holmes was born March 8, 1841.	10
He graduated from Harvard in 1861 and from Harvard	20
Law School in 1866. He was appointed a Justice of	30
the Supreme Court in 1902. He died March 6, 1935.	40

....1....2....3....4....5....6....7....8....9....10

5. **Test Your Skill:** *Take Three 2-Minute Timings.*
   Goal: 18 words a minute within 4 errors.
       Record your best speed within 4 errors.

WORDS

All the alphabet keys.

Skill and experience will get you the job but	10
very often are not enough to enable you to hold it	20
and advance. You must realize that in addition to	30
being a qualified worker, you must be pleasant too.	40

....1....2....3....4....5....6....7....8....9....10

Lesson 19: Horizontal Centering   **51**

ALPHABETIC SENTENCES

MARGINS: 10-75 (Pica)
20-85 (Elite)

Alphabetic sentences give you a thorough review of all the letters; they help you to gain perfect control of the keyboard. Type them at an even, steady pace—as accurately as you can.

Follow this routine:

1. Try a sentence a day—type it 10 times.
2. Practice the words that have errors.
3. Type the sentence 10 more times.
4. Start over when you have done them all.

WORDS:
```
     ....1....2....3....4....5....6....7....8....9....10...11...12
 1.  Jerry and Martha packed five dozen quilts in two huge boxes.
 2.  Felix Quope and Zeb Graves may cause a fire with their junk.
 3.  A showy trapeze artist quickly jumped over five green boxes.
 4.  That quip lazy Dick made about Jackie vexed a few neighbors.
 5.  Jack Pahlevy of Iraq found two big azure boxes of marijuana.
 6.  Jovial chemist Grub quickly froze a mixture of brown powder.
 7.  A lazy witness from Quebec vexed patient judge Walter Kache.
 8.  Jacqueline Wytbok purchased several fur rugs in mixed sizes.
 9.  Two big foxes quickly jumped over those lazy, sleeping dogs.
10.  Paul Van Weems, an expert glazier, quickly finished the job.
11.  The hazard of quack medicines will be exposed by Dr. Juvtig.
12.  Cy Jexon, a brainy wag, quickly solved the fish maze puzzle.
13.  They quizzed four experts about knowledge of juvenile crime.
14.  Macy will pack my box with five dozen jugs of liquid veneer.
15.  Hy Quiveg will systematize complex jobs and jack up profits.
16.  Marvin quickly packed the box with five dozen jugs for Iraq.
17.  Many extra quick flights to Brazil uncovered perfect jewels.
18.  Cy and Elza did  mix the big jar of soapy water very quickly.
19.  Five pale gray taxis whizzed by the Jonquin Steamship docks.
20.  Max Vidjub zips fingers quickly across keys without pausing.
     ....1....2....3....4....5....6....7....8....9....10...11...12
```

LESSON 20
VERTICAL CENTERING

Margins: 15-70 (Pica)
          25-80 (Elite)
Spacing: Single

1. **Review:** Type each line twice. Double space after each 2-line group.

```
Stew Quay Vina Phil Biff Drew Maxie Hugh Zora Jack
The friends a person buys are not worth the price.
f4 j7 f5 j6 d3 k8 s2 19 ;0 13 20 48 70 956 648,317
President John Adams was born on October 30, 1735.
Our invoice No. 14902 covers your order No. 37856.
```

Type invoice and order numbers without commas. (Line 5)

2. **Vertical Centering:** Vertical centering means typing material so that it appears with equal top and bottom margins.

A. Standard typing paper is 11 inches long.

B. Typewriters space 6 lines to the inch.

    So: A full sheet has 11 x 6 = 66 lines.

        A half sheet has $5\frac{1}{2}$ x 6 = 33 lines.

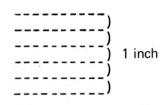

1 inch

To center material vertically:

(1) Count the typed and blank lines in the copy.

(2) Subtract the total lines from the number of lines available on your paper— 66 or 33.

(3) Divide the remainder by 2. The answer is the line number on which to start typing. Drop any fraction.

EXAMPLE A: *To center 25 lines on a full sheet:*

    (1) Subtract 25 from 66. Answer: 41.

    (2) Divide 41 by 2. Answer: $20\frac{1}{2}$. Drop the fraction.

    (3) Start typing on line 20 from top edge of the paper.

EXAMPLE B: *To center 12 lines on a half sheet:*

    (1) Subtract 12 from 33. Answer: 21.

    (2) Divide 21 by 2. Answer: $10\frac{1}{2}$. Drop the fraction.

    (3) Start typing on line 10 from top edge of the paper.

Number Keys

1	ala ala ala aql aql 1 lass 1 light 1 apple 1 quart
2	sw2 sw2 s2s s2s s2s 2 sets 2 sales 2 sacks 2 ships
3	de3 de3 d3d d3d d3d 3 dads 3 deals 3 dukes 3 drugs
4	fr4 fr4 f4f f4f f4f 4 furs 4 firms 4 flags 4 fires
5	fr5 fr5 f5f f5f f5f 5 feet 5 fines 5 files 5 farms
6	jy6 jy6 j6j j6j j6j 6 jobs 6 jeeps 6 jokes 6 jails
7	ju7 ju7 j7j j7j j7j 7 jugs 7 jumps 7 jokes 7 jacks
8	ki8 ki8 k8k k8k k8k 8 kits 8 kinds 8 kicks 8 kites
9	lo9 lo9 l9l l9l l9l 9 lads 9 lamps 9 lives 9 locks
10	;p0 ;p0 ;0; ;0; ;0; 10 pay 10 put 10 pals 10 pints

Symbol/Special Keys

$	f$f f$f f$f f$f Give her $40 or $41 or $42 or $43.
&	j&j j&j j&j j&j Macy & Web; Zale & Quig; Dix & Co.
%	f%f f%f f%f f%f I got 25%; Cy got 35%; Al got 40%.
#	d#d d#d d#d d#d We need 73# of #38 and 63# of #39.
( )	l(l l(l ;); ;); (one) (two) (three) (four) (five);
:	;:; ;:; ;:; Dear Al: Dear Hy: Dear Jo: Dear Ma:
?	;?; ;?; ;?; He? Who? Why? When? Which? Where?
/	;/; ;/; ;/; a/c d/c n/c c/o and/or we/they 2/3 5/8
½	;½; ;½; ;½; ½ of 60; ½ of 128; ½ of 394; ½ of 576;
¼	;¼; ;¼; ;¼; ¼ of 56; ¼ of 218; ¼ of 390; ¼ of 475;

Practice the drills for your machine: M *for* Manual; E *for* Electric

—	M	j_j j_j j_j j_j We <u>must</u> have <u>all the copies</u> today.
	E	;_; ;_; ;_; ;_; Your money is <u>refunded</u> in <u>10 days</u>.
¢	M	;¢; ;¢; ;¢; ;¢; pops 10¢; candies 20¢; franks 30¢;
	E	j¢j j¢j j¢j j¢j caps 26¢; horns 36¢; balloons 46¢;
@	M	;@; ;@; ;@; bags @ 20¢; boxes @ 30¢; cartons @ 90¢
	E	s@s s@s s@s bags @ 23¢; boxes @ 25¢; cartons @ 28¢
"	M	s"s s"s s"s s"s "wow" "sow" "slow" "show" "straw";
	E	;"; ;"; ;"; ;"; "pep" "pup" "plop" "prop" "plump";
'	M	k'k k'k k'k Dick's coat; Dick's scarf; Dick's pin;
	E	;'; ;'; ;'; Hap's tires; Hap's auto; Hap's garage;
*	M	;*; ;*; ;*; ;*; Sale lots are marked *; as 10* 20* 30*
	E	k*k k*k k*k k*k Sale lots are marked *; as 48* 58* 68*

Job 1 (Tryout)
Center on a
Full Sheet.

BUSINESS COURSES
Evening Classes

Write or Phone
For
Free Bulletin

*To leave one
blank line in
single-spaced
typing, use
the return
lever or
key twice.*

BERNARD M. BARUCH COLLEGE
17 Lexington Avenue
New York, New York 10010

Phone 673-7700
7 to 9:30 p.m.

Let us plan and center Job 1:

1. A. Clear the machine.
   B. Set a tab stop at the center of the paper.
   C. Set line-space regulator for single spacing.

2. A. Count the typed lines — 10
   B. Count the blank lines — 3
   Total lines in the advertisement — 13

3. A. Jot down the total lines in a full sheet — 66
   B. Subtract the total lines in the advertisement — 13
   Total lines left over for top and bottom margins — 53

4. A. Divide total lines left over by 2: $53 \div 2 = 26\frac{1}{2}$ or 26.
   B. Space down 26 lines from top edge of the paper.

5. A. Tabulate to the center of the paper.
   B. Backspace once for every 2 strokes in the first line.
   C. Type the line.
   Repeat these 3 steps till you have centered all the lines.

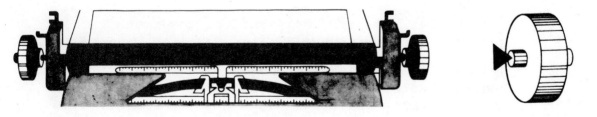

Fig. 17a. Aligning Scale   Fig. 17b. Variable Line Spacer

Aligning scale is on each side of the point where type bar strikes the paper. (See Fig. 17a) Make sure that top edge of the paper is even with top of aligning scale. Press in or pull out variable line spacer—the button in the left cylinder knob. Then return it to its normal position.

Lesson 20: Vertical Centering   **53**

KEYBOARD-MASTERY DRILLS

To help you master the keyboard, list the keys on which you often make errors. Then practice the drill for each key—until you can type it smoothly and accurately.

MARGINS: 15-70 (Pica)
25-80 (Elite)

Alphabet Keys:

A	aa	aAa	alarms	animal	appear	attain	awaken	aa	aAa
B	bb	bBb	babble	bribes	bubble	barber	blurbs	bb	bBb
C	cc	cCc	circus	circle	cracks	cactus	clutch	cc	cCc
D	dd	dDd	dawdle	addled	delude	deride	divide	dd	dDd
E	ee	eEe	evenly	events	evolve	energy	emerge	ee	eEe
F	ff	fFf	firths	fluffs	fluffy	offers	suffer	ff	fFf
G	gg	gGg	groggy	gauges	gorges	gargle	giggle	gg	gGg
H	hh	hHh	health	height	hyphen	hushed	higher	hh	hHh
I	ii	iIi	idioms	idiots	inning	incite	invite	ii	iIi
J	jj	jJj	jalopy	juggle	junior	jingle	jostle	jj	jJj
K	kk	kKk	kicker	knacks	knocks	kulaks	kopeck	kk	kKk
L	ll	lLl	lilies	lulled	loller	lolled	llamas	ll	lLl
M	mm	mMm	mimics	maxims	maimed	mammal	mammon	mm	mMm
N	nn	nNn	ninety	nonage	noncom	nation	Newton	nn	nNn
O	oo	oOo	oppose	oozing	onions	oblong	odious	oo	oOo
P	pp	pPp	pepsin	pepper	papers	poplin	poplar	pp	pPp
Q	qq	qQq	quirks	quacks	quaint	qualms	quarry	qq	qQq
R	rr	rRr	rumors	rivers	repair	rarely	return	rr	rRr
S	ss	sSs	shirts	sleeps	shreds	sister	series	ss	sSs
T	tt	tTt	tattle	taunts	taught	tattoo	tatter	tt	tTt
U	uu	uUu	udders	uncles	umpire	ultimo	Ursula	uu	uUu
V	vv	vVv	valves	velvet	vivify	vervet	Victor	vv	vVv
W	ww	wWw	winnow	widows	window	willow	Walter	ww	wWw
X	xx	xXx	exerts	taxing	X-rays	Xerxes	boxing	xx	xXx
Y	yy	yYy	yeasty	yellow	yearly	yonder	yachts	yy	yYy
Z	zz	zZz	zenith	zephyr	zigzag	zygote	pizzas	zz	zZz

3. **Practice:** Center Jobs 2, 3, and 4 vertically and horizontally.

Job 2
Center on a
Full Sheet.
(66 Lines)

```
TYPISTS

We Need You

EXCELLENT STARTING SALARY

Paid Vacations
Paid Holidays
Paid Health Insurance
Paid Sick Leave

BARTON CAREER AGENCY
137 West 42 Street
New York, New York

Call Miss Ostend
608-9501
```

Note: To center
vertically on a
half sheet, sub-
tract total lines
from 33

Job 3
Center on a
Half Sheet.

```
A HIGH SCHOOL DIPLOMA

Will Help You

To Get

A Better Job

STAY IN SCHOOL
```

Job 4
Center on a
Half Sheet.

```
SATURDAY
LUNCHEON

Chicken Gumbo Soup

Chopped Steak Sandwich
on Toast

Ice Cream or Fruit Cup
Milk or Coffee
```

Job 6

ALL-TIME HOME RUN HITTERS

Player	HR	League
Aaron	745	American
Ruth	714	American
Foxx	534	American
Williams	521	American
Ott	511	National
Mays	505	National
Gehrig	493	American
Mathews	477	National
Musial	475	National
Mantle	473	American

4. **Paragraph Practice:** Double Spacing.
   Try for a PERFECT copy of each paragraph:

		WORDS
All the number keys	Franklin D. Roosevelt, born January 30, 1882,	10
	became President March 4, 1933. He was re-elected	20
	in 1936, 1940, 1944. On August 14, 1941 he joined	30
	in drafting the structure of the Atlantic Charter.	40

....1....2....3....4....5....6....7....8....9....10

After the attack on Pearl Harbor, December 7,   10

1941, he began to plan for victory in World War 2.   20

In Axis aggression he saw a threat to our liberty.   30

He died at Warm Springs, Georgia, April 12, 1945.   40

....1....2....3....4....5....6....7....8....9....10

5. **Test Your Skill:** Take Three 2-Minute Timings.
   Goal: 18 words a minute within 4 errors.
      Record your best speed within 4 errors.

		WORDS
All the alphabet keys.	No type of job you have is worth while if you	10
	do the work lazily till quitting time. If you are	20
	eager to make good in business or any other field,	30
	get into the type of work in which you can put in	40
	full time and exert your best efforts for success.	50

....1....2....3....4....5....6....7....8....9....10

Job 4

AMERICA'S TALLEST BUILDINGS

Building	Location	Hgt., (Ft.)
Sears Tower	Chicago	1,454
World Trade Center	New York City	1,350
Empire State	New York City	1,250
Standard Oil	Chicago	1,136
John Hancock	Chicago	1,107
Chrysler	New York City	1,046

Job 5

NOBEL AWARDS IN LITERATURE

Name	Country	Year
Eyvind Johnson	Sweden	1974
Patrick White	Australia	1973
Heinrich Boll	Germany	1972
Pablo Neruda	Chile	1971
Aleksandr Solzhenitsyn	U.S.S.R.	1970
Samuel Beckett	France	1969
Yasunari Kawabata	Japan	1968

LESSON 21

NEW KEYS
¢ (Cents)   ½ (One-Half)

MARGINS: 15-70 (Pica)
 25-80 (Elite)
SPACING: Single

1. **Review:** Type each line twice. Double space after each 2-line group.

```
frvfb jujmn ftfg jyjh decd ki,k swxs lo.l aqza ;p/
The expert is one who excels in his chosen career.
f4f j7j f5f j6j d3d k8k s2s 19l ;0; ;-; ;:; ;/; ;?
On June 28, 1957, we flew to Brazil on Flight 360.
Zachary Taylor was born in Virginia Nov. 24, 1784.
```
All the alphabet and number keys.

2. **New-Key Practice:** ¢

A. *Manual Machine:* The ¢ is beside the ;-key. Use ;-finger. Practice the reach from ; to ¢ and back home to ;. Keep the **J**-finger in home position. When you can reach the ¢-key without looking at your fingers, type this drill twice:

No space between a number and the sign ¢.

```
¢ ¢ ¢ ;¢; ;¢; ;¢; Pay up to 7¢ or 8¢ or 9¢ or 10¢.
```

B. *Electric Machine:* The ¢ is on the **6**-key. Use **J**-finger. (1) Depress left shift key; (2) Reach for the **6**-key; (3) Zip fingers back home. Practice these steps until you can do them smoothly without looking at your fingers. Then type this drill twice:

```
¢ ¢ ¢ j¢j j¢j j¢j The items are 6¢, 16¢, 26¢, 36¢.
```

C. *Manual and Electric:* Type each line twice.

```
Ship 3 doz. at 20¢; 6 at 26¢; 8 at 30¢; 38 at 46¢.
Our items are marked 10¢, 36¢, 47¢, 59¢, 64¢, 93¢.
Jackie bought 5 oranges at 8¢; 6 at 9¢; 12 at 10¢.
Get 1 pair at 30¢; 3 pairs at 56¢; 8 pairs at 70¢.
Buy 15 stamps at 6¢; 7 at 8¢; 9 at 10¢; 14 at 12¢.
```
All the number keys.

3. **New-Key Practice:** ½   *Use ;-Finger.*

Practice the reach from ; to ½ and back home to ;. Keep the **J**-finger in home position. When you can reach the ½ without looking at your fingers, type each line twice:

No space between a number and the sign ½.

```
½ ½ ½ ;½; ;½; ;½; ½ hour; ½ week; ½ month; ½ year;
;½; ;½; ;½; The sum of 10½ and 15½ and 20½ is 46½.
Yes, 3 is ½ of 6; 4½ is ½ of 9; and 7½ is ½ of 15.
The swimming pool is 25½ feet long, 14½ feet wide.
I walked 2½ miles in a half hour; 4½, in one hour.
```

4. **Practice:** Test your skill. Center vertically and horizontally Jobs 2, 3, 4, 5, and 6, each on a full sheet.

Job 2

AMERICA'S FASTEST TYPISTS

Name	Words a Minute	Test Length
Ortiz Peters	120	45 minutes
Grace Phelan	133	30 minutes
George Hossfield	139	60 minutes
Albert Tangora	147	60 minutes
Margaret Hamma	149	60 minutes

Job 3

LARGEST CITIES OF THE WORLD

City	Population	Year
Tokyo	8,708,000	1974
Mexico City	7,768,000	1973
Peking	7,570,000	1970
New York	7,567,000	1974
Moscow	7,410,000	1973
London	7,349,000	1973

4. **Paragraph Practice**: Double Spacing.
   Try for 2 PERFECT copies of this paragraph:

	WORDS
We have the following orders to fill: 58 for	10
size 2½ at 14¢; 20 for size 3½ at 26¢; 78 for size	20
4½ at 17¢; 83 for size 5½ at 19¢; 35 for size 6 at	30
23¢; 50 for size 6½ at 27¢; 9 for size 10½ at 40¢.	40

....1....2....3....4....5....6....7....8....9....10

5. **Test Your Skill**: *Take Three 3-Minute Timings.*

Follow these steps in all your 3-minute timings.

A. Repeat if you finish before end of 3 minutes.
B. After each timing, jot down total words typed and total errors.
   Practice the words that have errors till they are easy for you.
C. Your 3-minute speed is words typed divided by 3.
D. Record on your 3-minute Score Sheet your best speed within 4 errors.
   Goal: 20 words a minute within 4 errors.

	WORDS
The mature person bears the accidents of life	10
with grace and dignity, making the best of things.	20
Your mind is like your stomach; it is not how	30
much you put into it, but how much you can digest.	40
The value of an education lies in the ability	50
to make a living out of the know-how you acquired.	60

....1....2....3....4....5....6....7....8....9....10

COMMON WORD COMBINATIONS

<u>Two Words</u>	<u>One Word</u>	<u>Compound Words</u>
all right	anywhere	by-product
any time	anybody	world-wide
every day	everywhere	well-known
no one	nowhere	follow-up

Step 1 is: **To Center the Tabulation Vertically**

Follow these steps exactly:

1. Jot down the number of lines available on a full sheet 66
2. Jot down the number of lines used in the tabulation: (6 typed and 6 blank) 12
3. Jot down the number of lines left over 54
4. Divide the number of lines left over by 2 (For top and bottom margins) 27
5. From the top edge of the paper, space down to line 27
   (13 double spaces and 1 single—turn cylinder up once)

Step 2 is: **To Center the Tabulation Horizontally**

Follow these steps exactly:

1. From the center of the paper, backspace once for every 2 strokes in the heading. The backspacing pairs are:
   CO/MM/ON/space W/OR/D space /CO/MB/IN/AT/IO/NS/   Then type the heading.
2. Space down 1 double and 1 single—to leave 2 blank lines below the heading. Then set the carriage at the center.
3. Select the longest entry in each column:
   1st: *Two Words* 2nd: everywhere 3rd: *Compound Words*. Backspace once for every 2 strokes in the 3 longest entries as though there were no spaces between them. The backspacing pairs are:
   Tw/o space/Wo/rd/se/ve/ry/wh/er/eC/om /po/un/d space/Wo/rd / Drop the s.
   Then backspace 6 more times—$\frac{1}{2}$ of the 6 spaces between columns 1 and 2; and $\frac{1}{2}$ of the 6 spaces between columns 2 and 3. Set the left margin stop when you finish backspacing. Column 1 begins at that point.
4. From the left margin, space once for each stroke in *Two Words* and 6 more times for the spaces between columns 1 and 2. Set a tab stop when you finish spacing. Column 2 begins at that point.
5. Space once for each stroke in "everywhere" and 6 more times for the spaces between columns 2 and 3. Set a tab stop when you finish spacing. Column 3 begins at that point.
6. Draw the carriage back to the left margin.
7. Type across the paper, tabulating from column 1 to column 2 and from column 2 to column 3.

Lesson 35: 3-Column Tabulations (With Column Headings)

LESSON 22

NEW KEYS
$ (Dollars)   ' (Apostrophe)

1. **Review:** Type each line twice. Double space after each 2-line group.

```
frvfb jumjh ftfg jyjh decd ki,k swxs lo.l aqza ;p/
Ray Fan Ted Hig Wes Vic Bob Max Pol Zoel Quen Jack
Those who know the least are least eager to learn.
;¢; ;¢; ;¢; Our pads sell at 4¢, 6¢, 8¢, 10¢, 12¢.
;½; ;½; ;½; The sum of 14½ and 25½ and 39½ is 79½.
```

Stretch the shift-key finger. Keep the others in typing position.

2. **New-Key Practice:** $ *Use F-Finger.*

The **$** is on the **4**-key. (1) Depress right shift key; (2) Reach for the 4-key; (3) Zip fingers back home. When you can do these 3 steps smoothly without looking at your fingers, type each line twice:

No space between the sign $ and a number.

```
$ $ $ f$f f$f f$f Give $40 or $41, not $45 or $46.
f$f f$f f$f Get the jar for $4; the jug for $4.50.
f$f f$f f$f Buy the jalopy for $400, not for $475.
My bill is $446.  My check is for $442.  I owe $4.
The diamond costs $450; the pearl, $40; send $490.
```

3. **New-Key Practice:** ' (Apostrophe)

A. *Manual Machine:* The ' is on the **8**-key. Use the **K**-finger. (1) Depress left shift key; (2) Reach for the **8**-key; (3) Zip fingers back home. When you can do these 3 steps smoothly without looking at your fingers, type this drill twice:

```
' ' ' k'k k'k k'k Is this Vicki's book or Luigi's?
```

Use apostrophe to indicate:
1. Ownership
2. Contraction
3. Feet
For exclamation mark:
Type a period. Backspace and type an apostrophe. Some machines have a special !-key.

B. *Electric Machine:* The ' is beside the ;-key. Use the ;-finger. Practice the reach from ; to ' and back home to ;. Keep the **J**-finger at home. When you can reach the ' without looking at your fingers, type this drill twice:

```
' ' ' ;'; ;'; ;'; It is Kip's job to fix Hap's car.
```

C. *Manual and Electric:* Type each line twice:

```
Hello Suzy:  Max saw Vicki's car in Jack's garage.
Ben couldn't wear Frank's hat; it wasn't his size.
Dixie is 4 3/4' tall; her brother Quill is 5 1/2'.
Don't pay $9 for the pin!  It isn't worth so much!
Marvin, you've done a good job!  I'm proud of you!
```

No space before or after an apostrophe within a word.

LESSON 35
3-COLUMN TABULATIONS
WITH COLUMN HEADINGS

1. **Review:** Type each line twice. Double space after each 2-line group.

Single Spacing.

```
abcd efgh ijkl mnop qrst uvw xyz ;? ;/ ;@ ;½ ;¼ ;--
cog fir kit lap man box jay via now dish quiz size
Things will come your way--when you go after them.
f4f j7j f5f j6j d3d k8k s2s l9l ;0; 12 34 56 78 90
We sold 210 shirts, 938 ties, 475 caps, 165 belts.
```

2. **Test Your Skill:** *Take Three 5-Minute Timings.*

Goal: 25 words a minute within 5 errors.

Record your best speed within 5 errors.

WORDS

Use double spacing.

	WORDS
The work of a secretary involves the handling	10
of office routine. She may be the personal assist-	20
ant of an executive, relieving him of many routine	30
tasks. Often she does work of an executive nature.	40
Here are some of the duties the secretary may	50
perform: read all incoming mail and draft replies	60
to routine letters; take dictation and transcribe	70
it on the typewriter; make appointments; interview	80
callers; order supplies; handle petty cash; write	90
checks and pay bills; verify bank statements; make	100
reservations in distant hotels. She must be ready	110
to perform daily a large variety of business tasks.	120

```
....1....2....3....4....5....6....7....8....9....10
```

3. **Tabulations with Column Headings:** Planning and typing a tabulation with column headings is just as easy as doing one without column headings.

A. Type each column heading even with the column. Underscore the column heading. Leave 1 blank line under it.

B. If the column heading is more than 5 strokes wider than the column, try to shorten it by abbreviating or changing certain words.

C. If the column heading is wider than the column, use it when you backspace for the horizontal centering.

Now, let us plan and type the tabulation in Job 1, page 104.

FIRST: Move the margin stops to the extreme ends; clear all tab stops; set line-space regulator at 2—for double spacing; insert a full sheet; center the carriage.

4. **Paragraph Practice:** Double Spacing.

Try for a PERFECT copy of each paragraph.

```
        Here is what it cost us to put our men on the     10
moon:  $1.1 billion for research; $3.3 billion for        20
designing; $9.4 billion for Saturn Rocket Engines;        30
$7.8 billion for spacecraft; and $2.25 billion for        40
salaries to scientists, office supplies, and help.        50
Total cost of the moon flight:  about $24 billion.        60
....1....2....3....4....5....6....7....8....9....10
```

```
        A boat is called a She because there's always     10
a gang of men around her; because there's always a        20
great deal of bustle about her; because she's very        30
often decked out; because it's not the initial ex-        40
pense that breaks you, it's the upkeep; because in        50
coming into port she's on the alert for the buoys.        60
....1....2....3....4....5....6....7....8....9....10
```

5. **Test Your Skill:** Take Three 3-Minute Timings.
   Goal: 20 words a minute within 4 errors.
   Record your best speed within 4 errors.

```
        Your typewriter has some kind of marker known     10
as the printing-point indicator.  It points to the        20
space on the scale at which the carriage is set to        30
type the next letter.  If the marker points to 50,        40
for example, the carriage is at the 50th space; so        50
the next key you hit will print in the 51st space.        60
....1....2....3....4....5....6....7....8....9....10
```

Job 6

AFRICAN NATIONS

Algeria	Guinea	Nigeria
Botswana	Kenya	Senegal
Burundi	Lesotho	South Africa
Cameroon	Liberia	Sudan
Zaire	Libya	Tanzania
Ethiopia	Malawi	Togo
Gabon	Mauritania	Tunisia
Gambia	Morocco	Uganda
Ghana	Niger	Zambia

LESSON 23
NEW KEYS
(Number or Pounds) & (Ampersand)

1. **Review:** Type each line twice. Double space after each 2-line group.

```
no so ham ego fun zip joy irk cur box led vow quit
f4f f$f f4f f$f I paid only $4.50 for this $8 hat.
k8k k'k k8k k'k Isn't this Mac's or Vic's sweater?
A gift of money is nice; it's so easily exchanged.
Robert's pay is $90 a week, but Stanley's is $100.
```

Eyes on copy. Be a touch typist.

2. **New Key Practice:** # The # is on the 3-key. Use D-Finger.
Practice the reach like this: (1) Depress right shift key; (2) Reach for the **3**-key;
(3) Zip fingers back home. When you can do these 3 steps without looking at your
fingers, type each line twice:

No space between the sign # and a number.

```
# # # d#d d#d d#d Ship Orders #30, #35, #37, #383.
d#d d#d d#d Pay Bills #3, #31, #32, #36, #38, #39.
Pack these in lots of 10#, 29#, 38#, 56#, and 74#.
d3d d3# d#d d#d The sign # means number or pounds.
We shipped 13# of #310 and 53# of #37 to the firm.
```

3. **New-Key Practice:** & *The & is on the 7-key. Use J-Finger.*
Practice the reach like this: (1) Depress the left shift key; (2) Reach for the **7**-key;
(3) Zip fingers back home. When you can do these 3 steps without looking at your
fingers, type each line twice:

One space before and after the sign &. Type policy numbers without commas.

```
& & & j&j j&j j&j Sax & Co., Vim & Zale, Mac & Co.
j&j j&j j&j Call Fox & Co., Gay & Co., Poe & Bond.
Ship at once Webb & Zorn's Order #350 for $492.68.
Mail invoices to Lux & Son, Quin & Co., Tyle & Co.
Joe's Policy #293648 was issued by Wexler & Smith.
```

Job 4

WHO INVENTED IT AND WHEN

Television	V. K. Zworkin	1928
Motion Pictures	Thomas Edison	1893
Safety Match	J. D. Lundstrom	1855
Saxophone	Adolphe Sax	1850
Sewing Machine	Elias Howe	1846
Telegraph	Samuel Morse	1837
Revolver	Samuel Colt	1835

Job 5

HEAVYWEIGHT BOXING CHAMPIONS

James J. Corbett	Max Schmeling	Rocky Marciano
Bob Fitzsimmons	Jack Sharkey	Ingemar Johansson
James J. Jeffries	Primo Carnera	Floyd Patterson
Tommy Burns	Max Baer	Sonny Liston
Jack Johnson	Jim Braddock	Joe Frazier
Jess Willard	Joe Louis	Jimmy Ellis
Jack Dempsey	Ezzard Charles	George Foreman
Gene Tunney	Joe Walcott	Muhammad Ali

4. **Paragraph Practice:** Double Spacing.
   Try for a PERFECT copy of each paragraph:

	WORDS
The symbol # typed before a figure stands for	10
the word number. When it is typed after a figure,	20
it stands for the word pounds. This symbol may be	30
used in technical work and in preparing invoices.	40

....1....2....3....4....5....6....7....8....9....10

	WORDS
The symbol & is used only when it is part of	10
the name of a firm. It is correct to write A & P,	20
A & S, Peck & Peck because these firms spell their	30
names this way. But to write Joel & Maxie is poor	40
style unless the reference is to such a firm name.	50

....1....2....3....4....5....6....7....8....9....10

5. **Test Your Skill:** Take Three 3-Minute Timings.
   Goal: 20 words a minute within 4 errors.
   Record your best speed within 4 errors.

	WORDS
The typewriter produced a vital change in our	10
social order because it enabled women to enter the	20
business world. Before the invention of the type-	30
writer, the only positions open to the ladies were	40
nursing and teaching. The typewriter opened up to	50
women the world over exciting careers in business.	60

....1....2....3....4....5....6....7....8....9....10

4. **Practice:** Test your skill. Center vertically and horizontally Jobs 2, 3, 4, 5, and 6, each on a full sheet.

Job 2

LONGEST RIVERS IN THE WORLD

Nile	Yellow River	Amur
Amazon	Yenisei	Lena
Mississippi	Parana	Mackenzie
Yangtze	Irtish	Niger
Ob	Congo	Mekong

Job 3

BASIC TYPEWRITER PARTS

Carriage	Line-space Regulator	Type Bar Guide
Carriage Scale	Margin Set	Shift Keys
Carriage Release	Paper Bail	Shift Lock
Carriage Return	Paper Guide	Space Bar
Cylinder	Paper Release	Backspacer
Cylinder Knobs	Paper Rest	Margin Release

LESSON 24

NEW KEYS
% (Percent)   ( ) (Parentheses)

MARGINS: 15-70 (Pica)
25-80 (Elite)
SPACING: Single

1. **Review:** Type each line twice. Double space after each 2-line group.

```
very buzz stew code flax ruse high main joke quips
d3d d3d d#d d#d The sign # means NUMBER or POUNDS.
We shipped 13# of #31 and 63# of #38 to Mr. Dixon.
j7j j7j j&j j&j The sign & indicates the word AND.
Wolfe & Ramsey delivered the items to Kepton & Co.
```

Release shift lock instantly after typing in all capitals.

2. **New-Key Practice:** %   The % is on the 5-key. Use F-Finger.
(1) Depress right shift key: (2) Reach for the 5-key; (3) Zip fingers back home.
Practice these steps till you can do them smoothly—without looking at your fingers.
Then type each line twice:

No space between a number and the sign %.

```
% % % f%f f%f f%f Pay 5%; Pay 6%; Pay 7%; Pay 10%;
f%f f%f f%f Tax of 2%, 3%, 4%, 5%, 6%, 7%, 8%, 9%;
f%f f%f f%f Get 5% or 6% interest on the $75 bond.
Max got 10%; Vic got 15%; Zoel got 25%; I got 50%.
Our 5½% rate on the $2,960 note is reduced to 4½%.
```

Keep elbows close to body.

3. **New-Key Practice: Left and Right Parentheses ( ).**

A. The left parenthesis is on the **9**-key. Use **L**-Finger.   (1) Depress left shift key;
(2) Reach for **9**-key; (3) Zip finger back home. When you can do these steps without looking at your fingers, type this drill twice:

```
l9l l(l l9l l(l l9l l(l l9l l(l l9l l(l l9l l(l
```

B. The right parenthesis is on the zero-key. Use ;-Finger. (1) Depress left shift
key; (2) Reach for zero-key; (3) Zip finger back home. When you can do these
steps without looking at your fingers, type this drill twice:

```
;0; ;); ;0; ;); ;0; ;); ;0; ;); ;0; ;); ;0; ;);
```

C. Now test your control. Type each line twice: Keep elbows close to body.

```
( ( ( l(l l(l l(l The ( is the shift of the 9-key.
) ) ) ;); ;); ;); The ) is the shift of the 0-key.
One (1); Two (2); Three (3); Seven (7); Eight (8);
The reference (the one on page 94) must be quoted.
July 4 is America's Independence Day (since 1776).
```

No space between parentheses and material within them.

CITIES OFTEN MISSPELLED

Abilene	Des Moines	Phoenix
Albuquerque	Houston	Poughkeepsie
Asheville	Los Angeles	Racine
Boise	Milwaukee	Schenectady
Chattanooga	Minneapolis	Tucson

Step 1 is: **To Center the Tabulation Vertically**

Follow these steps exactly:

1. Jot down the number of lines available on a full sheet 66
2. Jot down the number of lines used in the tabulation: (6 typed and 6 blank) 12
3. Jot down the number of lines left over 54
4. Divide the number of lines left over by 2 (for top and bottom margins) 27
5. From the top edge of the paper, space down to line 27
   (13 double spaces and 1 single—turn cylinder up once).

Step 2 is: **To Center the Tabulation Horizontally**

Follow these steps exactly:

1. From the center of the paper, backspace once for every 2 strokes in the heading. The backspacing pairs are: CI/TI/ES/space O/FT/EN/space M/IS/SP/EL/LE/ Drop the D. Then type the heading.
2. Space down 1 double and 1 single—to leave 2 blank lines below the heading. Then set the carriage at the center.
3. Select the longest entry in each column:
   1st: Albuquerque; 2nd: Los Angeles; 3rd: Poughkeepsie. Backspace once for every 2 strokes in the 3 longest entries as though there were no space between them. The backspacing pairs are:
   Al/bu/qu/er/qu/eL/os/space A/ng/el/es/Po/ug/hk/ee/ps/ie/
4. Backspace 6 more times—1/2 of the 6 spaces between columns 1 and 2; and 1/2 of the 6 spaces between columns 2 and 3. Set the left margin stop when you finish backspacing. Column 1 begins at that point.
5. From the left margin, space once for each stroke in Albuquerque and 6 more times for the spaces between columns 1 and 2. Set a tab stop when you finish spacing. Column 2 begins at that point. Space once for each stroke in Los Angeles and 6 more times for the spaces between columns 2 and 3. Set a tab stop when you finish spacing. Column 3 begins at that point.
6. Draw the carriage back to the left margin.
7. Type across the paper, tabulating from column 1 to column 2 and from column 2 to column 3.

Lesson 34: 3-Column Tabulations (Without Column Headings)   **99**

4. **Paragraph Practice:** Double Spacing.
   Try for a PERFECT copy of each paragraph:

WORDS

Did you know that in 1965 American women held	10
70% of all national wealth; 80% of all life insur-	20
ance benefits; 65% of all savings accounts; 48% of	30
all railroad stock; and about 23% of all the jobs?	40

All the numbers plus the new keys.

....1....2....3....4....5....6....7....8....9....10

Independence Day in the United States is July	10
4 (since 1776). July 4 is Independence Day too in	20
the Philippines (since 1946), and Venezuela (since	30
1821). In Argentina it is on July 9 (since 1810).	40

....1....2....3....4....5....6....7....8....9....10

5. **Test Your Skill:** Take Three 3-Minute Timings.
   Goal: 20 words a minute within 4 errors.
   Record your best speed within 4 errors.

WORDS

All typing beginners make errors. You are no	10
exception. So do not get the feeling that you are	20
clumsy with your hands whenever you strike one key	30
for another. Just shrug off those errors you make	40
and keep going. Typing is a skill that requires a	50
lot of repetitive practice. Everyone can learn to	60
type by touch. You only need a real zest to learn.	70

All the alphabet keys.

....1....2....3....4....5....6....7....8....9....10

Lesson 24: % ( ) (Parentheses)

LESSON 34

3-COLUMN TABULATIONS
(Without Column Headings)

MARGINS: 15-70 (Pica)
25-80 (Elite)

1. **Review:** Type each line twice. Double space after each 2-line group.

Single Spacing.

```
abcd efgh ijkl mnop qrst uvw xyz ;/; ;?; ;¢; ;½ ;-
deft jazz your view quip sure exam lone high backs
The sweetest sleep is after the alarm clock rings.
;¢; ;¢; ;@; ;@; The ¢ means cents; the @ means at.
;½; ;½; ;¼; ;¼; Get 10 @ 10¼¢; 20 @ 9¼¢; 30 @ 8¼¢.
```

2. **Test Your Skill:** Take Three 5-Minute Timings.

Goal: 25 words a minute within 5 errors.

Record your best speed within 5 errors.

	WORDS
Your tabulator is a great time-saver. Use it	10
for indenting paragraphs and other operations that	20
require you to zip the carriage to any scale point	30
you wish without repeatedly striking the space bar.	40
When you have set the tab stops, you need not	50
look for the tab bar or key to depress it. Use it	60
by touch. Simply hold it down until your carriage	70
has stopped. Then just continue with your typing.	80
Never strike the tab bar or tab key. To do so may	90
quite often put your machine entirely out of order.	100
Know your typewriter. Treat it well. That is the	110
only way to get the best possible service from it.	120

Double Spacing.

```
....1....2....3....4....5....6....7....8....9....10
```

3. **3-Column Tabulation:** Planning and typing a 3-column tabulation is just as easy as doing one with 2 columns. For the third column, you simply set another tab stop.

Let us plan and type the tabulation in Job 1, page 99.

FIRST: Move the margin stops to the extreme ends; clear all tab stops; set line-space regulator at 2—for double spacing; see that the paper guide is at 0; insert a full sheet; center the carriage.

LESSON 25

NEW KEYS
" (Quotation Mark) — (Underscore)

MARGINS: 15-70 (Pica)
25-80 (Elite)
SPACING: Single

1. **Review:** Type each line twice. Double space after each 2-line group.

```
we eve sir kin hug map fed tax cubs joys quay lazy
Parents can improve their children by loving them.
f5f f5f f%f f%f Vic got 40%, and Max got only 25%.
191 1(1 ;0; );) (one) (two) (three) (four) (seven)
Mr. Zuckor paid the tax (18% of his total income).
```
Correct posture avoids errors.

2. **New-Key Practice:** ” (Quotation Mark)

   A. *Manual Machine:* The ” is on the **2**-key. Use the right shift key and the **S**-finger. Practice the reach: (1) Depress right shift key; (2) Reach for the **2**-key; (3) Zip fingers back home. When you can do it smoothly without looking at your fingers, type this drill twice:

```
" " " s"s s"s s"s Maxie said, "Wow, a 3-base hit."
```

   B. *Electric Machine:* The ” is on the apostrophe-key. Use the left shift key and the semicolon-finger. Practice the reach: (1) Depress the left shift key; (2) Reach for the apostrophe-key; (3) Zip fingers back home. When you can do it smoothly without looking at your fingers, type this drill twice:

```
" " " ;"; ;"; ;"; He said, "Pat types quite fast."
```

   C. *Manual and Electric:* Type each line twice:

Double space after each 2-line group.

Use quotation marks to indicate: (1) Someone's words; (2) Titles; (3) Seconds. Apostrophe means minutes.

```
"Well," Ben asked, "will you introduce me to her?"
The teacher said, "Sit erect--as tall as you can."
Cal said he likes the rhythm in Poe's "The Raven."
Jim Ryun from Kansas ran an indoor mile in 3' 57".
The pugilist was knocked out in 2' 10" of Round 8.
```
No space between quotation marks and material quoted.

3. **New-Key Practice:** — (Underscore)

   A. *Manual Machine:* The — is on the **6**-key. Use **J**-Finger. (1) Depress left shift key; (2) Reach for the **6**-key; (3) Zip fingers back home. Practice these steps until you can do them smoothly without looking at your fingers. Then type this drill (next page) twice:

Job 6

OCCUPATIONAL BIRTHSTONES

Builders   Cornerstone
Burglars   Keystone
Laundrymen   Soapstone

Motorists   Milestone
Opticians   Grindstone
Pedestrians   Tombstone

Politicians   Blarney Stone
Stockbrokers   Curbstone
Shoe Repairmen   Cobblestone

_ _ _ _ j_j j_j_j_j <u>Underscore</u> words for <u>emphasis</u>.

B. *Electric Machine:* The — is on the hyphen-key. Use semicolon-finger. (1) Depress left shift key; (2) Reach for the hyphen-key; (3) Zip fingers back home. Practice these steps until you can do them smoothly without looking at your fingers. Then type this drill twice:

_ _ _ ;_; ;_; ;_; Paul Marx is an <u>accurate typist</u>.

C. *Manual and Electric:* Type each line twice.

Rule to remember: Space <u>twice</u> after typing colon.
<u>Promises</u> make friends, but <u>performances</u> keep them.
<u>Five most encouraging words</u>: "I am proud of you."
Remember: Quitters <u>never win</u>; winners <u>never quit</u>.
Women look for <u>bargains</u> but <u>never</u> for a <u>cheap man</u>.

4. **Paragraph Practice:** Double Spacing.
Try for 2 PERFECT copies of this paragraph:

	WORDS
The <u>Americans</u> characterize speech that is not	10
entirely clear by saying "That's Greek to me"; the	20
<u>Russians and Roumanians</u> by "That's Chinese to me";	30
the <u>French</u> by "That's Hebrew to me"; and the <u>Poles</u>	40
by "That's Turkish to me." All have the same idea.	50

....1....2....3....4....5....6....7....8....9....10

5. **Test Your Skill:** Take Three 3-Minute Timings.
Goal: 20 words a minute within 4 errors.
Record your best speed within 4 errors.

All the alphabet keys.

	WORDS	
The head of any business organization must be	10	*Use double spacing.*
careful in choosing among those who apply for jobs	20	
those men and women who are most likely to succeed	30	
in the business world. He is ever on the alert to	40	
recognize the applicants who have the exact traits	50	
required for the specific job and the ability that	60	
is sure to make them valuable members of the staff.	70	

....1....2....3....4....5....6....7....8....9....10

Job 4

WORDS OFTEN CONFUSED

accept	except
adjourn	adjoin
advice	advise
affect	effect
counsel	council
coarse	course
pale	pail
sale	sail
waste	waist

Job 5

CANNED PRODUCTS

Apricots	Orange Juice
Apple Sauce	Peas
Beets	Pickles
Blueberries	Pear Halves
Baked Beans	Peach Halves
Cherries	Spinach
Carrots	Spaghetti
Grapefruit Juice	String Beans
Lemon Juice	Tomatoes
Mixed Vegetables	Yams

LESSON 26

NEW KEYS

@ (At)   ¼ (One-Quarter)   * (Asterisk)

MARGINS: 15-70 (Pica)
25-80 (Elite)
SPACING: Single

1. **Review:** Type each line twice. Double space after each 2-line group.

```
wavy list neat axle quip jury from doze high back;
Any man can keep his word--if no one will take it.
s2s s2s s"s s"s We cannot use any "damaged" items.
j6j j6j j_j j_j Max subscribed to Tennis Magazine.
d3d d3d d#d d#d We need 13# of #31 and 63# of #37.
```

Reach for all top-row keys without looking up.

2. **New-Key Practice:** @
   A. *Manual Machine:* @ is on the ¢-key. Use left shift key and semicolon-finger. Practice the reach: (1) Depress left shift key; (2) Reach for the ¢-key; (3) Zip fingers back home. When you can do these steps without looking at your fingers, type this drill twice:

```
@ @ @ ;@; ;@; ;@; Get 30 @ 9¢; 40 @ 10¢; 50 @ 20¢.
```

One space before and after the sign @.

   B. *Electric Machine:* @ is on the **2**-key. Use right shift key and **S**-finger. Practice the reach: (1) Depress right shift key; (2) Reach for the **2**-key; (3) Zip fingers back home. When you can do these steps without looking at your fingers, type this drill twice:

```
@ @ @ s@s s@s s@s Get 90 @ 2¢; 62 @ 20¢; 72 @ 21¢.
```

   C. *Manual and Electric Machines:* Type each line twice.

```
The symbol @ means at or per; as 150 dozen @ 97½¢.
Ship 12 gross (1928) @ $80.65 (less 3½% discount).
Buy 10 @ 56¢; 125 @ 28¢; 374 @ 39¢; and 905 @ 68¢.
Send us 12 boxes @ 59¢ and another 12 boxes @ 60¢.
Try to ship 10 @ 16¢, 28 @ 47¢, and 30 @ 59¢ each.
```

3. **New-Key Practice:** ¼   *Use Semicolon-Finger.*
   The ¼ is on the ½-key. (1) Depress left shift key; (2) Reach for the ½-key; (3) Zip fingers back home. Practice these steps until you can do them smoothly without looking at your fingers. Then type each line twice:

No space between a number and the sign ¼.

```
¼ ¼ ¼ ;¼; ;¼; ;¼; ¼ hour; ¼ week; ¼ month; ¼ year;
For fraction ¼, hold left shift and hit the ½-key.
8 @ 1¼¢ is 10¢; 20 @ 2¼¢ is 45¢; 25 @ 3¼¢ is 81¼¢.
Order 10 more of size 29¼ and 50 more of size 39¼.
Yes, 12 is ¼ of 48; 16 is ¼ of 64; 30 is ¼ of 120.
```

4. Practice: Test your skill. Center vertically and horizontally Jobs 2, 3, 4, 5, and 6, each on a half sheet.

Job 2

WEDDING ANNIVERSARIES

Fifth	Wood
Tenth	Aluminum
Twentieth	China
Thirtieth	Pearl
Fortieth	Ruby
Fiftieth	Gold

Job 3

NEW EMPLOYEES

Abrams, Sam	Accountant
Azzinaro, Joe	Messenger
Carney, Vera	Clerk
Schultz, Nora	Typist
Shapiro, Sara	Stenographer
Thomas, Sue	Receptionist
Van Horn, John	Salesman
Watts, Donald	Buyer

4. **New-Key Practice:** *
   A. *Manual Machine:* The * is on the hyphen-key. Use semicolon-finger. (1) Depress left shift key; (2) Reach for hyphen-key; (3) Zip fingers back home. Practice these steps until you can do them smoothly without looking at your fingers. Then type this drill twice:

```
*  *  *  ;*;  ;*;  ;*;  Use the *asterisk for footnotes.
```

The asterisk may be put before or after a word.

   B. *Electric Machine:* The * is on the **8**-key. Use **K**-finger. (1) Depress left shift key; (2) Reach for **8**-key; (3) Zip fingers back home. Practice these steps until you can do them smoothly without looking at your fingers. Then type this drill twice:

```
*  *  *  k*k  k*k  k*k  Use the asterisk* for footnotes.
```

   C. *Manual and Electric:* Type each line twice. Double space after each 2-line group.

```
This symbol * is the shift of hyphen or the 8-key.
Special items are marked with the *; as, 50*, 68*.
The * directs you to extra text at bottom of page.
Jackie used the symbol * quite often in her essay.
When Prof. Broz* arrived, I requested him to wait.
```

All the alphabet keys.

5. **Paragraph Practice:** Double Spacing.
   Try for a PERFECT copy of each paragraph:

	WORDS
A Roman story tells of a tutor and his pupil,	10
a very young Prince. The lesson was in Roman His-	20
tory and the Prince was unprepared. "Now, we come	30
to the Emperor *Caligula" said the tutor. "Do you	40
know anything about him, Prince?" He didn't know.	50

```
....1....2....3....4....5....6....7....8....9....10
```

	WORDS
The tutor's question brought no response from	10
the Prince. The silence was getting embarrassing,	20
when it was broken by the tactful tutor, who said:	30
"Your Highness is right--perfectly right. For the	40
less said about the Emperor Caligula, the better."	50

```
....1....2....3....4....5....6....7....8....9....10
```

```
*A very cruel Roman Emperor born A. D. 12,
and assassinated by conspirators A. D. 41.
```

Lesson 26: @ (At) ¼ * (Asterisk)

BUSINESS ABBREVIATIONS

advt.	advertisement
amt.	amount
ans.	answer
bal.	balance
cwt.	hundredweight
doz.	dozen
misc.	miscellaneous

Let us plan and type the above tabulation.

FIRST: Move the margin stops to the extreme ends; clear all tab stops; set line-space regulator at 1; see that the paper guide is at 0; insert a half sheet; center the carriage.

Step 1 is: **To Center the Tabulation Vertically**

Follow these steps exactly:

1. Jot down the number of lines available on a half sheet 33
2. Jot down the number of lines used in the tabulation: (8 typed and 2 blank) 10
3. Jot down the number of lines left over 23
4. Divide the number of lines left over by 2 (for top and bottom margins) 11½
5. Drop the fraction. From the top edge of the paper, space down to line 11

Step 2 is: **To Center the Tabulation Horizontally**

Follow these steps exactly:

1. From the center of the paper, backspace once for every 2 strokes in the heading. The backspacing pairs are:
   BU/SI/NE/SS/space A/BB/RE/VI/AT/IO/NS/ Then type the heading.
2. Space down 3 times—to leave 2 blank lines below the heading. Then set the carriage at the center of the paper.
3. Select the longest entry in each column: Column 1: advt.   Column 2: advertisement
4. Backspace once for every 2 strokes in the 2 longest entries as though there were no space between them. The backspacing pairs are: ad/vt/period a/dv/er/ti/se/me/ nt/ Then backspace 3 more times—½ of the 6 spaces between the columns. Set the left margin stop when you finish backspacing. Column 1 begins at that point.
5. From the left margin, space forward once for each stroke in the longest entry in column 1 and 6 more times for the spaces between the columns. Then set a tab stop. Column 2 begins at that point.
6. Draw the carriage back to the left margin.
7. Type across the paper—from each entry in column 1 to the opposite entry in column 2. Hold down the tab key or the tab bar until the carriage stops at column 2.

Lesson 33: 2-Column Tabulations (Without Column Headings)   **94**

6. **Test Your Skill:** *Take Three 4-Minute Timings.*

Follow these steps in all your 4-minute timings.

A. Repeat if you finish before end of 4 minutes.
B. After each timing, jot down total words typed and total errors.
   Practice the words that have errors till they are easy for you.
C. Your 4-minute speed is words typed divided by 4.
D. Record on your 4-Minute Score Sheet (page 160) your best speed
   within 4 errors.
   Goal: 22 words a minute within 4 errors.

	WORDS
Do the work you have to do and do not clutter	10
your mind with trivia. It is unwise to quibble or	20
worry about the mistakes you made yesterday or the	30
problems you may have tomorrow. When you commence	40
a job no matter how small it is, see it through as	50
soon as you possibly can rather than having a half	60
dozen things dangling at one time. Get interested	70
in the task given you. Do it well. Soon you will	80
be assigned to more interesting and exacting work.	90

All the alphabet keys.

....1....2....3....4....5...6....7....8....9....10

LESSON 33
2-COLUMN TABULATIONS
(Without Column Headings)

MARGINS: 15-70 (Pica)
25-80 (Elite)

1. **Review:** Type each line twice. Double space after each 2-line group.

*Single
Spacing.*

```
frf juj ftf jyj fgf jhj ded kik sws lol aqa ;p; gh
fvf jmj fbf jnj dcd k,k sxs l.l aza ;/; ;¢; ;½; ;-
You can be almost anything that you resolve to be.
d3d d3d d#d d#d Ship order #30 for 153# of coffee.
k8k k8k k'k k'k Vicki's books are in Jack's house.
```

*Accuracy
is the
mark of
a good
typist.*

2. **Test Your Skill:** *Take Three 5-Mniute Timings.*
   Goal: 25 words a minute within 5 errors.
   Record your best speed within 5 errors.

	WORDS
Use double spacing. A tabulation shows the arrangement of data or	10
information in columns or tables. In the business	20
office, the typist is quite often required to type	30
a variety of data or information in columnar form.	40
Material prepared in columnar form is easy to	50
read and to understand. To the busy executive, it	60
is of immense help. It enables him to study, com-	70
pare, and interpret data much more quickly than if	80
the same material were arranged in paragraph form.	90
Now, plan and type the tabulation in Job 1, on the	100
next page. Follow each step exactly as explained.	110
Learn the routine; then you can center any tables.	120

```
....1....2....3....4....5....6....7....8....9....10
```

3. **Tabulation Tips:**
   A. Information typed in columns is a tabulation.
   B. Always center a tabulation horizontally. If it is typed on a half or full sheet without other matter, center it vertically and horizontally.
   C. Always leave 6 spaces between columns. Six spaces are equal to about ½ inch—an easy eye span in reading.
   D. Always type the heading in all capitals. Always leave 2 blank lines between the heading and the columns.

LESSON 27

PERSONAL LETTERS
BLOCKED AND SEMIBLOCKED STYLES

Margins: 15-70 (Pica)
25-80 (Elite)

1. **Review:** Type each line twice. Double space after each 2-line group.

Single Spacing.

```
abcd efgh ijkl mnop qrst uvwx yzab cdef ghij klmn;
There's always room at the top; too many fall off.
s2s s2s s"s s"s "One" "Two" "Three" "Four" "Five";
191 1(1 ;0; ;); (One) (Two) (Three) (Four) (Five);
I read (in The News Record) the article "Courage."
```

Keep hands and arms quiet; let the fingers do the work.

2. **Test Your Skill:** *Take Three 4-Minute Timings.*
   Goal: 22 words a minute within 4 errors.
   Record your best speed within 4 errors.

	WORDS
Double Spacing. Today you will apply your skill to the typing	10
of personal letters. These are the kind you write	20
to your family and friends. They are informal and	30
casual; they just talk to your family and friends.	40
The parts of the personal letter are: return	50
address, salutation, body, closing, and signature.	60
Always use white letter stationery, if available.	70
Type a neat, good-looking letter to show that	80
you think well of the one to whom you are writing.	90
Study the model on the next page and type a copy.	100

```
....1....2....3....4....5....6....7....8....9....10
```

PRINCIPAL BUSINESS JOBS

Bank Teller
Bookkeeper
Cashier

Order Clerk
Shipping Clerk   One blank line
Payroll Clerk   between groups.

Office Manager
Receptionist
Salesperson

Stenographer
Telephone Operator
Typist

3. **Letter Practice:** In the Blocked Style, paragraphs start at the margin. **Clear the** machine. Set a tab stop at the center of the paper—42 (Pica); 50 (Elite)—to spring the carriage to that point for the writer's address, date, and closing.

If your machine is Pica (large type), copy MODEL 1 *exactly*—line for line. If your machine is Elite (small type), type more words to the line—to have the side margins come out about equal. Listen for the bell.

MARGINS: 15-75 (Pica)
20-85 (Elite)
Start on line 15 from top edge of the paper.
Space 3 times after state before typing zip number.

MODEL 1
Short Personal Letter
Blocked Style
Single Spaced
Pica Type
Standard Punctuation

```
                          2830 Shore Road
                          Brooklyn, New York     11220
                          July 3, 1968
```

Salutation
on line 12
below date

```
          Dear Norma:

          Would you like to come along with me and mother on an
          auto trip to Bronxville? We're going to visit my aunt
          Beulah.  She said she would be happy to see you.
```

Body
of
Letter

```
          If you can go, put a few things in your suitcase and
          make yourself ready by 11 a.m., July 7. We'll pick
          you up in our car.  Tell mother and dad that we'll
          bring you home before noon, July 10.

                              Sincerely,
```

Leave 1 blank line before each paragraph and the closing.

Closing
(72 words)

Note: 1. No punctuation after writer's address and date; colon after the salutation; comma after the closing.

2. A short letter is one under 100 words. In such letters, start the salutation anywhere between 8 and 12 lines below date (depending on length of letter).

4. **Practice:** Test your skill. Center vertically and horizontally
   Jobs 2, 3, 4, and 5, each on a half sheet.

Job 2

FREQUENT LEGAL TERMS

Affidavit
Bankruptcy
Complaint
Eviction
Judgment
Plaintiff
Subpoena
Trespass

Job 3

HIGH SCHOOL SUBJECTS

Algebra
Biology
Chemistry
Commercial Law
English
French
Geometry
Italian
Physics
Spanish

Job 4

FAMOUS AMERICAN EXPLORERS

Roy Andrews
Robert Bartlett
Hiram Bingham
Daniel Boone
Richard Byrd
Kit Carson
William Clark
Frederick Cook
Lincoln Ellsworth
John Fremont
Meriwether Lewis
Robert Peary

4. **Letter Practice:** In the Semiblocked Style, paragraphs start 5 spaces from the margin. Set a tab stop at that point. If your machine is Pica, type MODEL 2 *exactly* —line for line. If your machine is Elite, type more words to the line—to have the side margins come out about equal. Listen for the bell.

MARGINS: 15-75 (Pica)
20-85 (Elite)

Start on line 15 from top edge of paper—at center.

MODEL 2
Average-length
Personal Letter
Semiblocked Style
Pica Type
Standard Punctuation

```
                               275 West 86 Street
                               New York, New York    10024
                               April 17, 1968
```

On line 8
below date

```
        Dear Ralph:

            Dr. William Brown, Director of Civil Defense at
        the Hudson Institute, will speak in Townsend Harris
        Hall, 138 Street and Amsterdam Avenue, next Thursday
        evening at 7:30, on the HUDSON INSTITUTE VIEW OF DIS-
        ARMAMENT.  The Hudson Institute makes studies of our
        national security.

            I am sure that you would like to hear this talk.
        Dr. Brown is a dynamic speaker.  He will have a mes-
        sage of interest to all City College graduates.

            The lecture will be followed by a discussion
        period.  It is sponsored by the City College Chapter
        of the Universities Committee on Problems of War and
        Peace.

            If you can make it that evening, phone me at my
        home before 5:30.

                        Sincerely,
```

(113 words)

Note: An average-length letter is one of 100-200 words. In such letters, start the salutation anywhere between 4 and 8 lines below the date (depending on length of letter).

```
                    Socrates
                    Plato
                    Aristotle
                    Martin Luther
                    Francis Bacon
                    John Locke
                    Jean Jacques Rousseau
                    Friederich Froebel
                    Herbert Spencer
                    Horace Mann
                    John Dewey
```

Let us plan and type the above listing.

FIRST: Move the margin stops to the extreme ends; clear all tab stops; set line-space regulator at 1; see that the paper guide is at 0; insert a half sheet; center the carriage.

Step 1 is: **To Center the Listing Vertically**

Follow these steps exactly:

1. Jot down the number of lines available on a half sheet 33
2. Jot down the number of lines used in the listing: (12 typed and 2 blank) 14
3. Jot down the number of lines left over 19
4. Divide the number of lines left over by 2 (for top and bottom margins) 9½
5. Drop the fraction. From top edge of the paper, space down to line 9

Step 2 is: **To Center the Listing Horizontally**

Follow these steps exactly:

1. From the center of the paper, backspace once for every 2 strokes in the heading. The backspacing pairs are:
FA/MO/US/space E/DU/CA /TO/RS/ Then type the heading.
2. Space down 3 times—to leave 2 blank lines below the heading. Then set the carriage at the center of the paper.
3. Select the longest entry in the listing: Jean Jacques Rousseau
Then backspace once for every 2 strokes. The backspacing pairs are:
Je/an/space J/ac/qu/es/space R/ou/ss/ea/ Drop the u.
4. Set the left margin stop when you finish backspacing. The column begins at that point.
5. Type the listing.

5. **Letter-Skill Test:** Below is a short unarranged personal letter. Type it 2 times: once in Blocked style, like MODEL 1; and once in Semiblocked style, like MODEL 2.

Remember: Listen for the bell—it rings when the carriage is 7 or 8 spaces from the right margin. When you hear the bell:

(1) Finish a short word—5 or fewer letters

or

(2) Divide a long word between syllables. Type a hyphen at the end of the line and finish the word on the next line.

SEE RULES FOR WORD DIVISION ON PAGE 130.

NOTE: If the keys lock and you need only 1 or 2 more spaces to finish the line, press the margin release key—at top of keyboard.

Home Address
Today's Date

Dear Maxie: Today we learned to type personal letters in the Blocked and Semiblocked styles.

In the Blocked style, paragraphs begin at the margin; in the Semiblocked style, they begin 5 spaces from the margin. Otherwise, both styles are alike.

Next week we learn to type business letters. As soon as I have done some of them, I'll send you samples.

So you did get that job you were after. Well, I hope you're happy now and doing well in it.

Sincerely,

(79 words)

LESSON 32
ONE-COLUMN LISTINGS

MARGINS: 15-70 (Pica)
25-80 (Elite)

1. **Review:** Type each line twice. Double space after each 2-line group.

Single Spacing.

```
frf juj ftf jyj fgf jhj ded kik sws lol aqa ;p; gh
fvf jmj fbf jnj dcd k,k sxs l.l aza ;/; ;¢; ;½; ;-
The real function of man is to live, not to exist.
s2s s2s s"s s"s "Look," he said, "here they come."
j6j j6j j_j j_j Mac did not say that she was late.
```

Use a sharp bounce-off tap on the space bar.

2. **Test Your Skill:** Take Three 5-Minute Timings.
   Goal: 25 words a minute within 5 errors.

   Record your best speed within 5 errors.

WORDS

Use double spacing.

```
     Every once in a while it is good to check up    10
on your typing technique.  Be sure that your pos-    20
ture in front of the machine is correct.  Correct    30
posture will aid you develop your typing skill at    40
a faster rate.  Keep your feet flat on the floor.    50
Sit erect as tall as you can and at perfect ease.    60
The chair should be the right height so that your    70
arms slant with your keyboard.  Keep elbows close    80
to your body; keep them quiet; let the fingers do    90
the work.  Keep eyes on the copy all the time and   100
return the carriage without looking up.  All this   110
sums up the rules by which to develop your skill.   120
....1....2....3....4....5....6....7....8....9....10
```

3. **One-Column Listing:**
   A. Material typed in one column is a listing; when typed in 2 or more columns, it is a tabulation.
   B. Always center a listing horizontally. If it is typed on a half or full sheet without other matter, center it vertically and horizontally.
   C. Always type the heading in all CAPITALS. Leave 2 blank lines between the heading and column.

PERSONAL BUSINESS LETTERS
BLOCKED AND SEMIBLOCKED

MARGINS: 15-70 (Pica)
25-80 (Elite)

1. **Review:** Type each line twice. Double space after each 2-line group.

Single Spacing.

```
abcd efgh ijkl mnop qrst uvwx yzab cdef ghij klmn;
jugs with the box five pack mode learn quick zippy
The wise man learns from the experience of others.
f4f j7j f5f j6j d3d k8k s2s 191 ;0; ;/; ;? ;¢ ;½;-
Read pages 2-20; 39-47; 56-64; 72-81; and page 93.
```

Try to type without pauses. Keep the carriage moving.

2. **Test Your Skill:** *Take Three 4-Minute Timings.*
   Goal: 22 words a minute within 4 errors.
   Record your best speed within 4 errors.

	WORDS
Double Spacing. A letter that you type to a place of business	10
is a personal business letter; it is much like the	20
personal letter that you practiced in the previous	30
lesson. In both letters, your return address, the	40
date, and the closing lines begin at the center of	50
the paper and are put in blocked form. But in the	60
personal business letter, you have to add the name	70
and address of the business house to which you are	80
writing. This part is known as the Inside Address.	90
Study the model on the next page; then type a copy.	100

....1....2....3....4....5....6....7....8....9....10

TWO-PAGE LETTERS

Most business letters require only one page. If a letter is too long for one page—

1. End the first page about one inch from the bottom. Make a light pencil mark 1½ inches from bottom. Type 3 more lines after reaching this mark.

2. End the page with a complete paragraph—if you can; if you cannot, leave at least 2 lines and carry over at least 2 lines to page 2.

3. On page 2, line 6 from top edge, type the addressee's name, the page number, and the date. These may be blocked at the left margin or spread evenly across the page. See models below.

4. Continue the letter on line 3 below the page 2 heading. Use the same line length as on page 1.

5. Use plain paper of the same size and quality as page 1.

```
Times Appliance Company, Inc.
Page 2
April 12,,1971


Your Instructions will be followed exactly.  Detailed
prices and a total for each part are listed.  We shall
```

Page 2 Heading, Block Form

```
Mr. Charles H. Andrews       2            June 6, 1971


    If the plans are changed, we shall submit a revised
list to you.  If the plans are not changed, we are ready
```

Page 2 Heading, Horizontal Form

3. **Letter Practice:** In the Personal Business Letter, you have to type the name and address of the person or company to whom you are writing. If your machine is Pica, Copy MODEL 3 *exactly*—line for line. If your machine is Elite, type more words to the line—to have the side margins come out about equal. Listen for the bell.

MARGINS: 15-70 (Pica)
25-80 (Elite)
SPACING: Single

MODEL 3
Short Personal
Business Letter
Blocked Style
Pica Type
Standard Punctuation

350 Chestnut Street
Akron, Ohio   44309
April 20, 1969

Start on line 15 from top edge, at center of the paper.

Start on line 8 below date.

Mr. Lester Thompson
Harmon Silk Co., Inc.
376 Montgomery Street
Akron, Ohio   44316

Dear Mr. Thompson:

About two months ago, I inquired by letter whether you could use an experienced stenographer with a knowledge of Spanish. You informed me that you had no opening then but that you would place my name on file.

Although I am now employed, I am still interested in working for your Export Division. You will note, by referring to my letter of application, that I have all the qualifications for the job and that I will make a good worker for you.

May I hear from you soon concerning the prospects of my joining your export staff?

Sincerely yours,

Irving Kantor

Typed name on line 4 below closing

(97 words)

4. **Letter-Skill Test:** Here are two average-length, unarranged letters. See whether you can arrange them attractively in the Full-Blocked Style. Use today's date.

Letter 1

Mr. John Clarkson, Manager/ Boyntex Auto Supplies, Inc./ 240 Madison Boulevard/ Milwaukee,/ Wisconsin 18107 Dear Mr. Clarkson: Within the next few months you may expect to receive requests for information concerning the new tubeless tires that have recently been developed. There will no doubt be a great demand for these tires because their many unusual features afford maximum riding comfort and ease of driving.

We plan to include in our stock a complete line of this superior product. There may be some delay, however, as manufacturers are having difficulty meeting the current demand.

A small shipment that may be used for display purposes should reach you this week. Please inform your customers that we shall do our best to fill their orders promptly./ Sincerely yours,/ HARMON TIRE COMPANY, INC./ George Rice/ Sales Manager   (106 Words)

Letter 2

Mr. William T. Ford/ Federal Insurance Company/ 283 Doyle Drive, Bangor,/ Maine 04401 Dear Mr. Ford: We are very sorry to learn that the public address system we installed two months ago has not been working satisfactorily. We assure you that we will correct this situation at once.

You realize that it is difficult for us to tell you the exact reason for its failure until we make a complete inspection. However, it is quite possible that some of the tubes are defective or that one of the loudspeakers is not in perfect condition.

As you suggested, one of our engineers will phone you next week for an appointment to visit you. At that time, he will make all necessary repairs. Yours truly,/ PUBLIC ADDRESS SYSTEMS, INC./ Henry J. Silver/ Chief Inspector
                                         (105 Words)

4. **Letter Practice:** If your machine is Pica, copy MODEL 4 *exactly*—line for line. If your machine is Elite, type more words to the line—to have the side margins come out about equal. Listen for the bell.

MARGINS: 15-75 (Pica)
20-85 (Elite)

MODEL 4
Average-length
Personal Business Letter
Semiblocked Style
Pica Type
Standard Punctuation

```
                          945 LaSalle Street
                          Chicago, Illinois    60607
                          July 17, 1969
```

Start on line 6 below date.

```
Hamilton Bags, Inc.
Attention Mr. Tom Galati
382 North Avenue
Chicago, Illinois    60609

Gentlemen:

     I am very much disappointed with your service in
filling my order of July 10 for a Blue Patent Leather
Handbag.

     The package reached me this morning.  When I ex-
amined the bag, I found that it was not the style I
ordered.  I specified Model DX, as advertised in THE
TRIBUNE, with my initials embossed under the snaplock.
You sent Model A, which is entirely too small for my
needs.  And it had no initials.

     So I am returning the bag to you today by insured
parcel post and would appreciate it if you will send
the correct bag promptly.  I am leaving on my vacation
July 30 and would like to have the bag by that time.

     Thank you for your attention to this matter.

               Sincerely yours,



               (Miss) Jane Murphy
```

(126 words)

3. **Letter Practice:** Copy Model 8 exactly—if your machine is Pica; if it is Elite, type more words to the line—to have the side margins come out about equal. Listen for the bell.

On Line 15

October 28, 19--

Start on Line 3 below date.

MODEL 8
Long Business Letter
Full-Blocked Style
Pica Type

Mr. Joseph Wagner
175 Turnpike Road
Boston, Mass. 02139

Dear Mr. Wagner:

Do you need extra money again this year?

You know from past experience that if you start selling Christmas Cards early, you make the most money. Your complete set of samples is ready and waiting for you. Again you will have the first opportunity to show your customers the best-designed and value-packed assortment in the greeting card industry.

Our FABULOUS FOILS Christmas Assortment contains 21 of the most beautiful cards you ever saw, and costs your customer only $2. These same 21 cards, if sold sepa- rately, cost up to 35 cents a card in any store. So you give your customer a $7.35 value for only $2.

You make $1 for selling 1 box; $2 for selling 2 boxes; $10 for selling 10 boxes; $50 for selling 50 boxes, etc., of our FABULOUS FOILS. Everybody buys at least 1 box of Christmas Cards. Many buy 4 and 5 boxes. So you make $1, $2, $3, $4, or more on almost every call. Last year, our records show, you made $102.

Your new sample kit, which we shall send you on approval, contains 4 boxes--all different. You may return them at our expense anytime within 20 days if you don't like them. As before, please send no money. Just fill in the card enclosed and mail it today.

Sincerely,

FABULOUS FOILS, INC.

Norman S. Kelvin
Sales Manager

(220 Words)

1 blank line

HC
Enclosure

5. **Letter-Skill Test:** Below is a short, unarranged Personal Business Letter. Type it 2 times: once in Blocked Style—like MODEL 3, and once in Semiblocked Style—like MODEL 4. Listen for the bell.

MARGINS: 15-75 (Pica)
20-85 (Elite)

Home Address
Today's Date

McClure & Rider, Inc.
920 Madison Avenue
New York, New York   10028

*Start on
line 12
below
date.*

Gentlemen:

May I ask a favor of you?

As secretary of the Advanced Typing Class
at Wadleigh Evening High School, Manhattan,
I am collecting a variety of successful
sales letters and circulars for display on
our BUSINESS BULLETIN BOARD.

Because your agency is so well known for
its effective advertising copy, I would
appreciate a few samples of your mail-order
letters and circulars.

Thank you for whatever material you can
furnish.

Sincerely yours,

(Miss) Emma Jones

(70 words)

LESSON 31

BUSINESS LETTERS
FULL-BLOCKED STYLE

Margins: 15-70 (Pica)
25-80 (Elite)

1. **Review:** Type each line twice. Double space after each 2-line group.

Single Spacing.

```
frvfb jumjh ftfg jyjh decd ki,k swxs lo.l aqza ;p/
A grudge is too heavy a load for anybody to carry.
f5f f5f f%f f%f I got 5%; Ben got 15%; Cy got 35%.
191 1(1 ;0; ;); (3) Three; (4) Four; (5) Five; (6)
Our interest (5%) and discount (2%) were accepted.
```

Use Finger-reach action only; keep hands and arms quiet.

2. **Test Your Skill:** *Take Three 5-Minute Timings.*

A. Repeat if you finish before end of 5 minutes.

Follow these steps in all your 5-minute timings.

B. After each timing, jot down total words typed and total errors. Practice the words that have errors till they are easy for you.

C. Your 5-minute speed is words typed divided by 5.

D. Record on your 5-Minute Score Sheet your best speed within 5 errors.

Goal: 25 words a minute within 5 errors.

	WORDS
Another style of business letter used by many	10
businessmen is known as the "Full-Blocked" letter.	20
In this style, all lines begin at the left margin.	30
The spacing between the parts of the letter remain	40
the same as in the blocked and semiblocked styles.	50
The "Full-Blocked" letter style is quite easy	60
and quick to type--no positioning of the date line	70
and no paragraph indenting. Typists and business-	80
men too, like these two time-saving features which	90
help produce more work and reduce office expenses.	100
Study the model on the next page; then type a copy.	110
....1....2....3....4....5....6....7....8....9....10	

Use double spacing.

LESSON 29
BUSINESS LETTERS
BLOCKED STYLE

MARGINS: 15-70 (Pica)
25-80 (Elite)

1. **Review:** Type each line twice. Double space after each 2-line group.

Single Spacing.

```
move text zone snow quip jury from sold high barks
The love for money is a love that never grows old.
f4f f4f f$f f$f The checks are for $4, $6, $8, $9.
k8k k8k k'k k'k Isn't the name O'Mara, not O'Neil?
Cal's note for $750 to John O'Leary is due May 12.
```

Use the correct finger for each top-row key.

2. **Test Your Skill:** *Take Three 4-Minute Timings.*
   Goal: 22 words a minute within 4 errors.
   Record your best speed within 4 errors.

	WORDS
Double Spacing.　A business letter is typed on a letterhead--a	10
sheet of paper 8½ by 11 (usually) with the company	20
name and address printed at the top. The two most	30
popular styles are called Blocked and Semiblocked.	40
In the Blocked style, each line begins at the left	50
margin, except the date and closing lines. In the	60
Semiblocked style, each paragraph is indented five	70
spaces from the left margin. With this exception,	80
both styles of business letter are quite the same.	90
Study the parts of a business letter on next page.	100
....1....2....3....4....5....6....7....8....9....10	

4. **Letter-Skill Test:** Below are two average-length, unarranged letters. See whether you can arrange them attractively in the Semiblocked Style. Use today's date.

Letter 1

Mr. James T. Reid/ Acme Realty Company/ 394 Seventh Avenue/ Atlanta, Georgia 31403 Dear Mr. Reid: In response to your request, we shall be glad to submit an estimate for installing two elevators in the new apartment house you are building at 286 Park Boulevard. We are happy to have this opportunity to serve you and will mail an itemized bid by the end of next week.

Although our bid may not be the lowest you receive, may we ask that you consider these facts before awarding the contract: We have been in business in this city for over 60 years and manufacture a high-grade product. We enjoy a reputation for excellent workmanship. Furthermore, our one-year guarantee provides complete and regular inspections.

If you decide to deal with our concern, we assure you of thorough satisfaction. Yours truly, SWEM & CO., INC. Samuel Hoffman, Chief Engineer   (122 Words)

Letter 2

Bryant Hardware, Inc./372 Farragut Street/ Philadelphia, Pennsylvania 19142 Gentlemen: Thank you for your interest in our Luxor Fans. Our representative, Mr. Fred Karlin, has been instructed to call on you within ten days. Mr. Karlin will make a definite appointment by telephone.

Our booklet listed only 60-cycle models because this is the type most commonly ordered. However, we can supply 40-cycle motors in any model without extra charge. Mr. Karlin will discuss this matter with you in detail.

All reports indicate that when hot weather comes there will be a strong demand for the new Luxor Fans with their durable motors and attractive colors. Demand should result in increased profits, and we want you to have your share. Sincerely yours, LANE ELECTRIC COMPANY/ George Flexner, President   (111 Words)

PARTS OF A BUSINESS LETTER

MODERN LOCKS, INC.
150 Park Avenue
Waco, Texas 76701

Letterhead: Printed name and address of the company.

March 8, 19--   *Date*

Smith & Whitman, Inc.
78 James Street
Detroit, Michigan 34205

Inside Address: Name and address of the company to whom letter is written.

Gentlemen: *Salutation:*

Here is an illustration of the new Snap-Lock we have developed. It has many new improvements.

Please insert this page between pages 19 and 20 of the catalog you now have. Our new catalog will be mailed to you as soon as it is ready.

Body: The letter itself. Letters are usually single-spaced, with one blank line between paragraphs.

Yours truly,   *Complimentary close:*

MODERN LOCKS, INC.   *Company name:* typed in all CAPITALS

3 blank lines for writer's signature

Sales Manager   *Writer's title*

JS:RK
Enclosure

Reference initials: Writer's and typist's
Enclosure reminder: Typed when something is enclosed with the letter

PLACEMENT OF LETTER

Margins: 15-75 (Pica) *For*
20-85 (Elite) *All*
Date: On Line 15 From top *Letters*

SIZE OF LETTER	WORDS IN BODY OF LETTER	SPACES BETWEEN DATE AND INSIDE ADDRESS	
Short	Up to 100	8 to 12	*Depending*
Average	100 to 200	4 to 8	*on length*
Long	Over 200	3 to 6	*of letter.*

3. **Letter Practice:** In the Semiblocked Style, paragraphs begin 5 spaces from the left margin. You already have a tab stop for paragraph indentions which you set for the 4-minute timings. Now, set another tab stop at the center—for the date and the closing lines. Type a copy of MODEL 7.

MODEL 7   December 12, 1969
Average-length
Business Letter
Semiblocked Style
Pica Type
Standard Punctuation

        Allen Screvane & Sons
        738 Van Alston Avenue
        Los Angeles, California   90017

        Gentlemen:

            We are enclosing a check for $375 to be credited
        to our account. We had expected to pay the full amount
        when the invoice became due and regret that we are un-
        able to send you a larger amount at this time.

            You will recall that the shipment of topcoats did
        not reach us until two weeks after the date on which
        you promised delivery. This caused a delay in the dis-
        play of our stock, which resulted in a slowing up of
        sales. Collections, too, are still poor in this town.
        Accordingly, we shall be unable to pay the balance of
        this account before the first of next month.

            We hope you will realize the position we are in
        and grant us this extension.

                            Sincerely yours,

                            PERRY BROTHERS, INC.

        GH:DW   Credit Manager
        Enclosure

                                    (123 Words)

3. **Letter Practice:** In the Blocked Style, all lines begin at the margin, except the date and the closing lines. Clear the machine. Set a tab stop at the center of the paper— for the date and closing lines. If your machine is Pica, copy MODEL 5 *exactly*—line for line. If your machine is Elite, type more words to the line—to have the side margins come out about equal. Listen for the bell.

MODEL 5   February 10, 1969   *Start on*
Short Business Letter   *line 15—*
Blocked Style   *at center.*
Pica Type
Standard Punctuation

Start on   Mr. O. V. Poole
line 12   409 East 35 Drive
below date. Wichita, Kansas   67202

       Dear Sir:

       Your credit reputation is probably your most valuable
       asset. Yet you are jeopardizing your credit rating
       for $79.38, the balance of your account with us.

       Since you have ignored our previous four letters, there
       seems to be no alternative for us except to turn this
       matter over to our attorneys.

       You can make this action unnecessary by mailing your
       check in the enclosed stamped envelope.

If the   Yours truly,
writer's
name is   *1 blank line*
not typed,   STAR GOODS CO., INC.
type his
initials   *3 blank lines*
first; then
yours.   Vice-President
       RW:JN
       Enclosure

                                     (67 words)

LESSON 30

BUSINESS LETTERS
SEMIBLOCKED STYLE

MARGINS: 15-70 (Pica)
25-80 (Elite)

1. **Review:** Type each line twice. Double space after each 2-line group.

Single Spacing.

```
fix save them power black quilt money amaze judges
To be calm under stress is the real sign of power.
d3d d3d d#d d#d Item #3 is for 3#; #39 is for 13#.
j7j j7j j&j j&j Webb & Sons buy from Smith & Zale
Mail Invoice #358 for 73# of sugar to Vukaj & Son.
```

Depress shift key firmly.

2. **Test Your Skill:** *Take Three 4-Minute Timings.*
   Goal: 22 words a minute within 4 errors.
   Record your best speed within 4 errors.

	WORDS
You have learned that in the blocked style of	10
business letter all the parts are started from the	20
left margin, except the date and the closing lines.	30
You start these lines at the center of your paper.	40
The semiblocked style of letter is almost the	50
same as the blocked style. The only difference is	60
that here you have to set two tab stops: the first,	70
five spaces from your left margin--to indent every	80
paragraph; the second, at the center of the paper,	90
for the date and the closing lines. Take a moment	100
to study the model on the next page; then type it.	110

Double Spacing.

```
....1....2....3....4....5....6....7....8....9....10
```

4. **Letter Practice:** Copy MODEL 6 *exactly*—if your machine is Pica; if it is Elite, type more words to the line—to have the side margins come out about equal. Listen for the bell.

MODEL 6   August 2, 1969   *Start on*
Average-length   *line 15—*
Business Letter   *at center.*
Blocked Style
Pica Type
Standard Punctuation

Start on   Mrs. Norma Meyers
line 8   856 Leonard Street
below date. Newark, New Jersey   07102

               Dear Mrs. Meyers:

               Thank you for your letter of July 27. We are pleased
               to hear from you and enclose the catalog you desire.
               It describes in detail the new line of appliances now
               on display in our showrooms.

               Our stock includes the finest brands with a guarantee
               for 90 days. For a limited time only, many items are
               now being offered at greatly reduced prices. There
               is just a small charge for labor when we make an in-
               stallation in your home.

               If you wish any further details about the equipment we
               carry, you may call or visit our sales office between
               the hours of 9 to 5 daily except Sunday. We suggest
               that you make your choice now in order to benefit from
               our summer clearance prices.

                              Cordially yours,

If the   DIX APPLIANCE CO., INC.
writer's
name is
typed, use
only your   Thomas Benardo
initials.   RJ   General Manager
               Enclosure
                                          (125 Words)

5. **Letter-Skill Test:** Below are two short, unarranged letters. See whether you can arrange each on a separate sheet in Blocked Style. Listen for the margin bell.

Letter 1

Today's Date / The Graphic Magazine/ 725 Clary Street/ Fort Worth, Texas 76112/ Gentlemen: Will you please cancel our advertising contract in your publication to take effect immediately.

Business conditions have compelled us to curtail a considerable portion of our advertising appropriation for the next six months.

Much to our regret, we must eliminate the magazines from our list./Yours truly, /MARVIN & MAXWELL, INC./ Jack Samuels/ Advertising Manager   (45 Words)

Letter 2

Today's Date / Mr. Sidney Harris/ 1756 Leewood Drive/ Hartford, Connecticut 30943/ Dear Mr. Harris: Our records show that the bill covering final charges of $27.50 for your gas and electric service has not been paid.

We shall appreciate prompt payment of this bill so that the account may be closed. Payment may be made by mail or in person at any Intercounty Lighting Company office. It is important that you clear up this amount before you move./ Yours sincerely,/ INTERCOUNTY LIGHTING COMPANY/ Vincent Kendall/ Collection Department   (63 Words)